A REGIONAL BOOK

OUR
Superlative
Pacific Northwest

ANN SALING

ANSAL PRESS
Edmonds, Washington

BOOKS BY ANN SALING
  Our Superlative Pacific Northwest
  The Foundations of Fiction
  Article Writing: a Creative Challenge
  Rhubarb Renaissance: A Cookbook
  The Carrot Cookbook

Copyright © Nov. 1984   by Ann Saling
Second Edition, completely revised, 1986

ISBN: 0-910455-01-5
Library of Congress CIP #: 83-071500

Published by
ANSAL PRESS   8620 Olympic View Drive
Edmonds, WA 98020
(206) 774-4645

Manufactured and printed in the U.S.A.

CONTENTS

ACKNOWLEDGMENTS

Many superlative Pacific Northwest people helped with the second edition of this book. I remember you all with gratitude, as I do those who helped with the first edition.

A special **merci** to Louise Berg, my Portland cousin, for her legwork on the first edition; to Roland Anderson of Seattle Aquarium, who made so many valuable suggestions; to Faith Deuprey who helped on the second edition in many ways.

Gracias to Helen Nieberl for proofreading the second edition; to Sally and Phil Webster for always being there when I needed computer help.

Arigato to the Seattle Library for their Quick-Information service.

And **obrigada** to Scott Forslund and Peter Potterfield of PACIFIC NORTHWEST Magazine for the assignment that was the germ of this book.

ART CREDITS

KARL MOLNER: full-page original drawings made for this book: cover, 9, 21, 33, 45, 57.

RICK D. SALING, my grandson: drawings for section pages 7, 85; drawings: 25, 47, 117.

FAITH DEUPREY: Back-cover sketch; drawings: 15, 27,30,31,34,36,38,41,51,59,68,79,82.

MAXINE MORSE: 14,39,43,48,69,75.

SHARON TORVIK (OREGON WILDLIFE): 11,12,19,23,35.

VIRGINIA V STEAMER FOUNDATION: drawing, 153, 155.
RICHARD AMUNDSEN: wildlife painting (photo), 49.

All uncaptioned photographs are by author.

A WORD FROM THE AUTHOR

Anyone familiar with the Pacific Northwest knows that this is an exceptionally beautiful part of the world-- wild rivers, dense forests, roadless wilderness, abundant wildlife, soaring mountain peaks, unspoiled ocean beaches.

Pride of place is equally strong in those who were born here and chose to remain, and in those of us born elsewhere who chose the Northwest as our home. The intention of this book is to put a foundation of fact beneath our pride of place, to list the superlatives-- the largest, the smallest, the oldest, the deepest-- of our three Pacific Northwest states: Oregon, Idaho and Washington. But this book is more than a mere Book of Records, barebones statistics. Its aim is entertaining enlightenment, with interesting facts provided about each of the superlatives.

A superlative can, of course, be negative: catastrophes, monster moles, record rainfall. But such undesirable aspects of Pacific Northwest life paradoxically enhance the quality of our life here. They may discourage the faint of heart from overpopulating our paradise.

Sometimes the measuring unit in ranking a superlative will be the Pacific Northwest; sometimes, that vast area west of the Mississippi; at other times, it may be the nation or the Western Hemisphere. More often than many of us realize, we can point with pride to something in our area unequaled in the entire world.

Alaska, Hawaii, and British Columbia are not included in this book, although each has its own superlatives. We share some of these. Since animals, plants, and geology do not respect political boundaries, some of our wonders spill over into neighboring territory, and some of theirs spill over into ours. We should take equal pride in the superlatives of each of the three states. Each is a unique part of this wonderful region, the Pacific Northwest.

PART ONE

THE ANIMAL WORLD

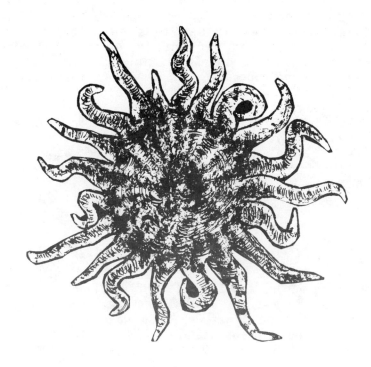

THE MOST UNUSUAL

1. CRANE: The most spectacularly unusual behavior of any Pacific Northwest bird is the dance of the greater sandhill crane (<u>Grus canadensis tabida</u>). Although once believed to be a courtship dance, and always most spectacular when performed by a mating pair, the dance may be only a nervous reaction to disturbance. It may be done at any time by all ages, even by 3-day-olds.

Birds may dance alone, or in couples, while others ignore them. Large groups may pair off to dance. With wings partly spread, the dancers quickstep around each other, silent or calling noisily, bowing heads, leaping as high as eight feet, making sudden stops. Sometimes they toss up vegetation or sticks, trying to catch them with their long, straight bill.

The cranes are our tallest Pacific Northwest bird, one of the tallest in the world, three to five feet high, with very long neck and legs. Strong flyers with a five- to seven-foot wingspan, they may fly over mountains as high as 14,000 feet when migrating. Often they call in flight in a deep, resonant voice. Very gregarious except when breeding, they usually stay in flocks.

Once plentiful from the Arctic to the Gulf of Mexico, they were driven to the Pacific Northwest and to Canada by intensive hunting and by the draining and cultivation of their wetlands.

The largest and densest breeding population in North America is at Grays Lake National Wildlife Refuge (NWR) in southeastern Idaho. In the spring some 250 nesting pairs and 600 non-breeders gather there; in the fall, about 2500.

At Grays Lake, the cranes, the only crane to breed in the western U.S., have been successful foster parents to more than three dozen whooping crane chicks. In 1985 27 eggs were sent to the Grays Lake sandhill cranes for incubating.

2. SLUG: Two slugs with most unusual and very unsluglike behavior live only in the Pacific Northwest, which may have the world's densest slug population. (Our soil is too acidic for large snails to form shells.) The Pacific Northwest has the only North American slug (Prophysaon obscuran) that can, when roughly handled, detach one-third of its tail end. This it can regenerate within five weeks. This species, which hibernates for nearly half the year within decaying logs, lives only on high mountains.

Another unusual Pacific Northwest slug (Hemphillia dromedarus) is one of only three mollusks in the world to display a "startle reaction" when handled. To escape predators, it will twitch and writhe, lash its tail and even jump an inch or two. Cold-adapted, it often is found near glaciers, on the Olympic Peninsula, in the Cascades near Portland up to 4250 feet, and in ravines of the Columbia River Gorge.

Another of our slugs (Arion ater rufus) will curl into a ball when in danger, and roll back and forth. When swallowed by a bird, it may block the bird's throat and suffocate it, later crawling out, still alive.

3. MOUSE: The red tree mouse (Phenacomys longicaudus) has the most unusual habitat and diet of any Pacific Northwest mouse. This mouse lives high in the fir trees in coastal Oregon and extreme southwestern Washington. Rarely found on the ground, the species is relatively unstudied. These small, sure-footed rodents move slowly, balancing with a three-inch-long tail that makes up more than half their total length.

They eat only conifer needles, using the resin ducts and midribs for nests, in which they give birth. The gestation period is longer, litters are smaller (1-3), and development of young slower than in other mice, perhaps a result of poor diet.

THE MOST PRIMITIVE

1. MOUNTAIN BEAVER: The mountain beaver (Aplo-dontia rufa) is the most primitive and ancient of living rodents, sole survivor of a family with 30 known fossil species. Neither beaver nor ex-clusively mountain dweller, the rabbit-sized rodent, with dense, dark brown fur once prized by Indians for robes, spends most of its time in its network of tunnels, dug with long, straight, sharp claws. Solitary and usually nocturnal, it often travels by tunnel to food sources, even at night. The tunnel complex, up to 5 feet deep and 6 inches in diameter, has rooms for nesting, for winter food storage, and for feces and garbage. Nearly blind, the mountain beaver moves molelike along the passages, aided by long whiskers. Clues to the many entrances, often hidden in brackens, matted brush, or blackberries, lie in piles of stones and dirt, and drying "hay."

The mountain beaver's primary predators-- mink and weasel-- may pursue the "boomer" through its tunnels. Usually silent, the animal "booms" when disturbed or angered. It has a strong musky odor.

The shy animals are found in Oregon and Washington on Cascade slopes as high as 9000 feet, and in moist lowland valleys and ravines, usually in second-growth areas, with deep easy-to-dig soil.

The stubby-tailed vegetarian relishes fern stalks, many shrubs, sprouts and seedlings, often standing upright to nip them off. Its preference for seedlings and future Christmas trees has led Oregon growers to encase the tiny trees in special plastic net tubes for protection.

2. DRAGONFLY: One of the world's most primitive dragonflies (<u>Tanypterayx hageni</u>) lives only in the Pacific Northwest. The black-and-yellow insect burrows into Washington bogs in the Olympics and Cascades. It is a relict of ancient dragonflies. Although all dragonflies are primitive and cannot close their wings at rest, this one differs from other dragonflies in laying eggs in bogs. Its larvae are terrestrial, not aquatic.

The largest prehistoric insect known was a dragonfly ancestor of 150 million years ago. One found in Permian rocks in Kansas had a wing span of $2\frac{1}{2}$ feet. Airplane designers study dragonfly flight because the insect can hover, fly sideways and even backwards, with 3 times the lift of the most advanced aircraft. Their maximum flying speed is 50 mph. University of Colorado aerospace engineers studying dragonfly aerodynamics photograph them tethered to harnesses in a wind tunnel.

Dragonflies have the best compound eyes of any insect, with 29,000 facets in each eye.

3. SNAKE: The most primitive of Pacific Northwest snakes, the rubber boa (<u>Charina bottae</u>), is our only boa. Secretive and gentle, the slow-moving snake, 30 to 34 inches long, has a rubbery body covered with small scales.

Rubber boas, very rare in logged areas, prefer well-drained, partly forested areas. When attacked, they play possum or coil up as if ready to strike, waving the tail and hiding the look-alike head under their body. Their tails often bear scars made by predators.

Like all boas, the rubber boa, which can swim, climb trees, and burrow into forest debris, kills by tightening its coils around small prey, suffocating and then swallowing it whole.

THE SMALLEST

1. SHREW: The pygmy shrew (Microsorex hoyi Washingtoni) is North America's smallest mammal. At less than four grams and 3 inches, it has probably reached the lower size limit for mammals. It is found only in Washington's northeast corner in semi-arid pine woods.

It utters high-pitched squeaks while poking in forest debris with its long snout, making sudden starts and stops, disappearing down tunnels a half-inch across. Disagreeable skin secretions make shrews unpalatable to many predators.

It has poor eyes, sharp teeth and a voracious appetite, seldom resting, always eating. Besides insects, the pygmy may eat berries and seeds, and even other animals, biting them in the neck.

2. OYSTER: The world's smallest edible oyster is the native Pacific Northwest Olympia oyster (Ostrea lurida), only two inches long. Gourmets consider the oysters, back from near-extinction in 1983, the world's best in taste, delicate in flavor. 500, shelled, make a quart.

Once plentiful all along the Pacific coast, they are now grown mostly in southern Puget Sound, in diked beds always covered by water.

Soon after their discovery in Willapa Bay in 1850 by New England oystermen who engaged in bitter oyster wars, the oysters were exploited for San Francisco's Gold Rush trade. In 1853 sailing ships carried 21,000 bushels to San Francisco.

Overharvesting ended the oyster boom about 1875. The nearly fatal blow came with the opening of a pulp mill in Shelton in the 1920s. After the mill closed, the bay was so polluted by sulfite wastes that nearly 25 years passed before the tiny oysters began to reproduce well again.

3. WEASEL: A Pacific Northwest subspecies of the short-tailed weasel (Mustela erminea Olympicus) is North America's smallest true carnivore. The male measures only 6 to 7.5 inches and weighs 1.5 to 2 ounces. The female is smaller.

The densely furred Olympic Peninsula weasel, dark reddish-brown above and white below, is unusual among weasels in not turning white during the winter. Sharp-eyed, courageous, active both day and night, this weasel catches and kills prey larger and heavier than it is, biting them repeatedly in the neck.

Slim, long-bodied, muscular, the short-limbed weasel can slip through mouseholes or knotholes. A good swimmer and climber, this efficient predator tirelessly pursues its prey, into crevices and holes, through water, up trees, over logs, onto rockpiles. It may kill more than it can eat. The weasel relishes mice, fish, frogs, moles, birds and eggs.

4. MOLE: The world's smallest mole, the shrew-mole (Neurotrichus gibbsi) lives only in the Pacific Northwest. A mere 2½ to 4½ inches long, including its scaly tail with bristly hairs, the shrew-mole may weigh no more than 2/5 of an ounce.

More common in Washington than in Oregon, the shrew-mole is found in dense moist lowlands, and in western ravines and on mountain slopes.

The size of a small shrew and somewhat resembling one, the shrew-mole is a true mole, with broad forefeet, long claws for digging, and a sensitive pointed snout. Probably descended from the shrew, moles are shrew-like in their very high metabolism rate. Day and night, seldom resting, the shrew-mole searches for food. Although almost blind, it forages on the surface, sniffing about with its snout, tunneling in decaying vegetation. It is never found in home gardens.

THE LARGEST

1. CLAM: The geoduck (Panopea generosa) is the largest clam in North America, and perhaps the world's largest intertidal burrowing bivalve. The nearly rectangular shell can reach 8 to 10 inches.

Age is measured by daily rings or lines in a polished and etched cross-section of shell. The record is 115 years, but growth probably stops at about 20 years. A three-pounder (commercial size) is 10 to 13 years old; six-pounders are common and 10-pounders are not rare.

Although the clams are found from Alaska to Baja California, Puget Sound has the only geoduck fishery in the nation, and the world's densest concentration of the clams, some 300 million pounds in southern Puget Sound. Geoducks are delicate in flavor, used raw in sashimi and sushi, fried in steaks, and cooked in soup and chowder.

After a month-long, free-floating stage, the geoduck settles down for life in a burrow it digs before its digging foot atrophies. Since the siphon of a nine-inch-long geoduck can stretch to three feet, the clams are usually found three to four feet deep. The Pacific Northwest Indian word, gueduc, means "dig deep." Even fully contracted, the siphon cannot fit inside the shell. As it contracts, it can squirt a powerful jet of water.

Found by diggers mostly at extreme low tides, geoducks are numerous in water 18 to 60 feet deep in beds more than ¼ mile offshore. In such deep beds, divers may see hundreds of siphons extended several inches above the sandy substrate they prefer, sucking in plankton.

2. CHITON: The world's largest chiton, the gum-boot, (<u>Cryptochiton stelleri</u>) lives in Pacific Northwest waters, home to many smaller species of chitons. The giant chiton, up to 18" long and 6" wide, is completely covered by a long, reddish-brown girdle, thick and leathery. The girdle conceals eight typical overlapping, calcareous plates which are often found on beaches as butterfly-shaped shells. They allow the chiton to roll up into a "sea cradle," protecting its soft parts.

Chitons, the most primitive of today's mollusks, are similar to fossils 400 million years old. The reduced head has only light-receiving and tactile cells, no eyes or antennae. Nocturnal and sluggish, chitons graze by scraping tiny algae off rocks with a snail-like radula. During the day most cling tightly with the broad ventral foot to a favorite rock, usually below tideline.

3. SLUG: The Pacific Northwest's largest land mollusk is the native banana slug (<u>Ariolimax columbianus</u>), which reaches 8 to 10 inches during its 7-year life. This mushroom-loving forest slug, often olive-colored and spotted with black, is not a pest. It is even useful. The spores of some mushroom species must pass through the digestive system of a slug before they will germinate.

4. FLEA: The largest flea in the world (<u>Hystrichopsylla schefferi</u>) was found in 1913 in the nest of its preferred host, a mountain beaver near Puyallup, Washington. Most adult fleas are about 0.03 inch long; this one was 0.31", the diameter of a pencil. A number of fleas are highly host-specific. For example, fleas parasitic on subterranean hosts such as moles, shrews and mountain beavers usually have very reduced eyes.

5. SCALLOP: The largest swimming scallop in the world, the weathervane (<u>Pecten caurinus</u>), is found in Pacific Northwest waters. The thin, fan-shaped shells (valves) are distinctly ribbed and 8 to 10 inches across. These scallops lie in beds with muddy or sandy bottoms in deep off-shore water. Unlike most bivalves which rest erect on the shell edge, the weathervane lies on its right valve, which becomes deeper than the upper valve with broader, flattened ribs. The upper valve of most Pacific Northwest pectens normally is covered by yellow sponges found nowhere else (<u>Mycale adherens</u> and <u>Ectyodoryx parasitica</u>).

Lacking a siphon, scallops filter food through the frilled mantle edge. The mantle is dotted with dozens of beadlike eyes, each with lens and retina but sensitive only to shadows and large objects

To escape danger, this scallop swims with open edge forward, taking in water, then expelling it as it repeatedly opens and snaps shut the valves. It moves fast enough to escape starfish but not octopus.

6. BARNACLE: Thriving in Pacific Northwest waters is <u>Balanus nubilus</u>, the world's largest acorn barnacle. It can grow 6 inches high with a 4-inch base diameter. When crowded, especially in deep water, individuals may grow on top of each other in a fragile tube a foot long. The Puget Sound giants are usually subtidal, often in deep water with strong, food-bearing currents.

Barnacles are one of the most highly modified crustaceans. Inside the conical shell, whose shape resists the force of water, is a shrimp-like creature, upside-down and waving, through the top opening of its shell, six pairs of bristly jointed legs. These feeding legs sweep through the sea, forming a basket that traps tiny crustaceans and organic fragments. They fold back, scraping food off onto the combs of the mouth parts. Then the food is ground up by bony jaws and swallowed.

The free-swimming barnacle larva, once it de- cides on a suitable place to settle-- often in a barnacle colony-- must complete within 12 hours a drastic metamorphosis. While battered by surf or ocean currents, it secretes first a glue (one of the strongest known), then six interlocking plates to form a shell house around the soft body. That superglue is being studied for use in dental fill- lings and in mending broken bones.

Once housed, the larva reorganizes its tissues into adult form with head and appendages, and attaches itself permanently inside its shell at the back of the neck. The barnacle is the only sedentary crustacean.

To grow, barnacles must expand their shell house. Again, the mantle that lines the interior of the shell secretes material it takes from the sea. The plates of the shell grow both upward from the base and also along the margins of each plate.

Barnacles, which usually live 3 to 5 years (a few live to 25 years) tolerate temperature changes very well. Retaining moisture inside the closed shell, they stay quiescent. Some, exposed on rocks that are covered only several times a month by extreme high tides, survive the dry periods tightly closed, taking in no food or air.

Barnacles have the longest penis in the world relative to the animal's size. The slender and extensible tube penetrates neighboring shells.

Many predators-- snails, starfish and some birds-- attack barnacles for the succulent flesh, also relished for centuries by Northwestern coast- al Indians. The dogwhelk covers the barnacle with its foot and forces the valves open. A predacious snail crawls onto the barnacle, and forces the valves apart by prying with a spine on its shell. It then inserts its probosis, and dines very well.

7. OCTOPUS: The world's largest octopus (<u>Octopus dofleini</u>) thrives in frigid Pacific Northwest waters, especially in Puget Sound. Commercial fishermen sometimes catch giants over 100 pounds. A 165-pound octopus was caught at Sequim Bay. An octopus estimated to weigh 300 pounds was pulled to a boat on a set-line after it had eaten three dogfish from the line. Too large to hoist aboard without damage, the octopus was released. Some years ago parts of a cut-up octopus led the Tacoma Aquarium director to speculate that the live octopus weighed 250 pounds.

Along with squid, the octopus is the most highly developed mollusk, with well-developed brain, eyes, and nervous system.

Nocturnal, shy, intelligent, curious, friendly, the octopus is seldom seen in open water. It holes up in dark caves or rocky crannies whose opening it may cover with stones or debris. With strong, sensitive, suckered arms, it feels for food, inserting an arm into a cranny or darting out to seize a fish or a passing crab, one of its favorite foods. It kills by first injecting a paralyzing toxin, biting the prey with the horny beak that lies within the arms

Although the octopus can travel by jet propulsion when necessary, it commonly uses its arms to move along the bottom or even to crawl out onto beach rocks after prey. It tires too easily to use jet propulsion for long.

Both male and female die young, at about three or four years of age. The male dies soon after fertilizing the female's eggs, the female soon after her carefully tended eggs hatch.

8. EAGLE: The bald eagle (<u>Haliaetus leucoce-</u><u>phalus</u>) is the Northwest's largest bird of prey at longer than 3 feet, with a 7-foot wingspan. Graceful in the air, they are often seen in the Pacific Northwest, soaring high in great circles.

Nowhere else in the world can so many people so easily observe so many bald eagles so near such a major metropolitan area as Seattle. Transients are easily glimpsed in the Skagit River Bald Eagle Natural Area not far from Seattle. That area, now totaling 924 acres, is one of the five most significant bald eagle wintering areas in the lower 48 with a peak of 300, varying with weather.

Although endangered or threatened in all the lower 48 states, the birds are gaining in numbers. Bald eagle population for the lower 48 is around 12,000 and increasing. Washington has the most bald eagles outside of Alaska-- some 1500 to 1800 with about 150 mating pairs. A few even nest within Seattle city limits.

All 3 Pacific Northwest states have relatively large wintering bald eagle populations. Oregon shares the largest group-- 500 to 600-- with California in the Klamath Basin National Wildlife Refuge. Bear Valley NWR is a major night roosting site used by as many as 300 eagles in one night. Oregon's large number of waterfowl refuges with many marshes, lakes and rivers provide ample food that attracts wintering eagles. '

Most of Idaho's 600 bald eagles winter at Lake Coeur d'Alene (36 gather at Wolf Lodge Bay), and near American Falls Reservoir.

The Skagit bald eagles are attracted by the high numbers of spawned-out chum salmon which die and are washed up on Skagit River gravel bars. The presence of suitable nesting trees in the area attracts the birds, which prefer large, old-growth Douglas fir or pine for nesting, sheltered from wind and with open tops that aid landing and take-off. Bald eagles use snags for watching for prey, resting, and cleaning plumage.

Bald eagles construct the largest nest of any bird in the world. The world record nest, which may have weighed two tons, measured almost 9½ feet across and 20 feet deep. Since the stick nests are added to each year-- with such novelties as a stalk of corn with ears still on it-- a nest can become heavy enough to break down a tree.

Relatively social, bald eagles roost together at night, soar together and often feed together. At night, in the always-warmer roosting sites, adults and juveniles are very vocal.

Although they mate for life, they quickly obtain a new mate when one dies. Nests may be used by different eagles for many years; a pair may use more than one nest in a season. Not very territorial with their own species, they fiercely defend their nests against predators.

More scavenger than predator, bald eagles feed on rodents, foxes, waterfowl, as well as fish. They may harass an osprey flying off with a fish, catching it in mid-air after it is dropped.

A heavy rabbit population on Washington's San Juan Island provides road-kills for the largest group of bald eagle nests within any area of equal size in the lower 48. The islands have resident eagles as well as wintering transients.

9. SNAIL: The largest intertidal rock snail of the Pacific Coast, with the handsomest shell in the Pacific Northwest, is the Oregon triton (Fusitriton oregonensis). Usually subtidal and found in water as deep as 300', the snail is found closer to shore on rocky coasts. Its spiraled shell is 6" long. Coarse bristles completely cover 7 or 8 ribbed whorls. It lays eggs, corn-kernel size and shape, in a spiral. The first-born in each capsule eat the others.

10. SALAMANDER: The Pacific Northwest is home to the world's largest terrestrial salamander, the Pacific Giant (<u>Dicamptodon ensatus</u>). A single species, it lives in all 3 Northwest states, but is largest and most abundant in Washington's Olympic Peninsula, where it reaches more than 12". It has a rounded snout, thick tapering tail, large mouth and heavy-set body.

Although most salamanders are voiceless, able to make only air-generated clicks, this giant produces an unusual variety of sounds: rattles, yelps and screams. It is also unusual in climbing trees and shrubs, 8 feet up, either for food or escape.

The giant prefers humid coastal forests near cold streams. Seldom seen during the day, it spends its time under logs, rocks and river bank overhangs. Some never leave the water. Displaying a unique salamander trait, <u>neoteny</u>, these individuals retain such larval characteristics as small legs, flat tail and external gills. Yet they are sexually mature, able to reproduce.

11. ANEMONE: In Pacific Northwest waters the white plumose sea anemone (<u>Metridium senile</u>) grows to be one of the largest sea anemones in the world-- 2 feet tall. Delicate and lovely, it extends into the water many feathery tentacles, usually white, which catch tiny organisms and bring them to the mouth opening. Larger animals that blunder into the tentacles are held, slowly turned and digested gradually.

Sea anemones are one of the most familiar of tidepool animals when expanded into a flowerlike shape, but unattractive lumps when tentacles are withdrawn in bright sunlight or at low tide. Also

common on floats and the lowest intertidal rocks,
they attach their basal disk so firmly they cannot
be removed without damage. Yet by muscular con-
tractions, they can glide on their basal disk some
18 inches in 24 hours.

Sea anemones are among the most primitive of
multicelled animals. They can reproduce by split-
ting in half, and, when food is scarce, decrease
in size and grow more slowly. Age is difficult to
estimate, but a captive sea anemone lived for 70
years, and in the ocean, they may live for 500.

They are among the most specialized of polyp-
type coelenterates, with well-developed nerve and
muscular networks. These "flower animals" respond
to mechanical danger and bright light or lack of
water by pulling the mouth disk with its tentacles
inside the column, which can be shortened, and
then closing the opening like a drawstring pouch.

Tentacles, mouth and column bear stinging
cells that paralyze most small animals touching
them. One kind of stinging cell is found only on
tentacles and disk; another, all over the animal.

Food captured by the tentacles is brought inside the column by a water current moved by down-
ward-beating flagella. A set of upward-beating
flagella creates an outgoing current that carries
waste out the same opening. When the tentacles
signal a catch, those flagella, in a complex
muscular reaction, reverse the direction of beat
to aid with food entry.

12. STARFISH: The world's largest and most active starfish, the sunflower (Pycnopodia helian-
thoides) grows up to 3 feet across in Pacific
Northwest waters, which have the world's largest
number and diversity of starfish species.

The broad-disked, soft-bodied sunflower, found
only on the Pacific Coast, is strikingly colored,
often salmon-pink with mottled gray and touches of
violet. Since the huge, soft body needs support,

adults are subtidal.

Born with 5 rays, the sunflower adds more in pairs. Although 24 rays are usual, up to 44 have been counted. The soft rays, easily torn off, can be regenerated if lost. A ray detached with part of the disk will form a new seastar.

Underneath, on the flexible tapering arms, are some 40,000 muscular tubefeet with suction-cup ends, the most highly developed foot of any echinoderm. The feet extend hydraulically and retract by muscles, moving the seastar along at a fast 6 to 8 feet a minute. Each tubefoot works independently and is weak, but together, the pull is 9 pounds a square inch, enough to force open a bivalve. The echinoderm water vascular system is unique, a single system serving for feeding, locomotion, respiration and for maintaining pressure and shape.

Suction cups at the tapered tentacle ends are modified; each tip has an eyespot and chemical-sensitive sensors that smell food.

Since seastars breathe through the thin skin, they must keep it free of debris. Hairlike cilia covering the upper surface move constantly, creating currents that disperse sediment. Tiny jaws on ball-and-socket joints seize any debris that settles and the current carries it away.

Most seastars eat by humping over a bivalve, forcing the valves open, and inserting part of the extruded stomach. The voracious sunflower actively digs for clams, ending up after a few days down in a pit, arms sticking up around the edges. It also feeds by sucking up into its ventral mouth whole prey-- purple sea urchins, barnacles, moon snails, small clams. Shells are discarded later. Most animals flee in panic at the approach of this seastar. Seastars have few predators except for gulls, sea otters and other seastars.

13. MOLE: Townsend's mole, (<u>Scapanus</u> <u>townsendi</u>), North America's largest, burrows only in the Northwest, especially in moist coastal areas of Washington and in the fertile Willamette Valley. The giant, which has very broad forefeet, measures up to nine inches, plus a two-inch tail.

Although seldom found in home lawns and gardens, Townsend's mole is a serious pest in Oregon and Puget Sound farmlands. During the rainy season a single mole can make up to 500 mounds one foot across at three-foot intervals. In spring a male, searching for a mate, can bulldoze 50 yards an hour, Except for a brief mating season, moles are fiercely independent. Even moles hate moles.

Almost wholly subterranean, they are highly specialized for underground life, nearly blind, with powerful breast muscles and forepaws like shovels. Passage along their tunnels is aided by lack of hips and external ears. Velvety fur without a set lets moles quickly reverse direction.

Active all year long, moles live at lower tunnel levels in winter, eating from huge caches of worms, kept alive after being disabled by a nip. Expert engineers, they are quick to repair a collapsed roof or to make a detour tunnel.

16. SNAIL: The world's largest species of moon snail (Polinices lewisii) is found in the Pacific Northwest on protected sandy mudflats and beaches. Where there are clams, there are often moon snails. Voracious feeders, they are seldom seen because they spend most of their time under the surface, searching for clams. The rounded shell, four to six inches long, has one main whorl and several small ones. It moves easily through sand, propelled by a huge fleshy foot.

That foot, when extruded, almost covers the shell but can be quickly pulled inside by draining water through holes at the edge of the foot. Then it is drawn into the shell, covering the opening. But the snail, lacking oxygen, cannot live long inside the closed shell.

As the snail excavates 1 to 12" deep in sand, it may leave surface ridges.

This most efficient burrower of all gastropods kills clams, mussels and other snails either by drilling a hole in the shell with its rasping tongue and sucking out the tissues, or by suffocating the animal with its huge foot and then opening the shell. In oyster beds, the moon snail is a serious pest, its huge foot smothering the young as it burrows for clams.

Its eggcase-- sand collar-- is often seen on the surface, 6" across, 3½" wide. Rachel Carson called it "a doll's shoulder cape." The snail extrudes its eggs between two folds of the foot in a gelatinous sheet that encircles the shell. Mucus and sand cement the eggs into a rubbery mass that holds together until the larvae hatch. The egg case disintegrates, washing larvae into the sea.

Hermit crabs use the large moon snail shells, often so heavy from all the debris and barnacles covering them that the crab can hardly move.

15. GAME FISH: Washington, Oregon, and Idaho share honors for world-record fish caught with rod and reel.

1. MOUNTAIN WHITEFISH. 1983. 5 lbs., 2½ oz., 41½". Unlimited-line class, caught on 8-lb. test line. Columbia River near Vernita Bridge.
2. LINGCOD. 1985. 56 lbs., 8 oz. Strait of Juan de Fuca.
3. KOKANEE. 1975. 6 lbs., 9.75 oz. 24½'. Priest Lake, Idaho.
4. MACKINAW. 57 lbs., 6 oz. Priest Lake, Idaho.
5. DOLLY VARDEN-- bull trout. 1949. 32 lbs. 40½". Pend Oreille Lake, Idaho.
6. STRIPED BASS. 1983 18 lbs., 12 oz. Not a world record, but the largest ever caught on such light tackle-- 4-lb. test line. Coos Bay, Oregon.

18. GIANT SQUID: The first giant squid (<u>Archi-teuthis</u>) caught off the Oregon Coast (1978) was the only whole one ever caught off the Pacific Coast north of Chile. This is the largest squid genus and the world's largest invertebrate animal. The giant weighed 225 lbs. and measured 24', arm tip to arm tip, across the five-foot-long body.

The genus was believed not to inhabit North-west waters. This one, caught by a commercial fisherman trawling for bottom fish off Mack Arch in southern Oregon, was alive when trawled at 800 feet. Only live flesh bruises, and several arms of the still-fresh body were bruised as they were thrust through the net. But nothing survives the rapid pressure change as nets are hauled up.

The fisherman, Gary Steffensmier, brought the squid ashore, and had it weighed, measured and photographed. Then he gave it to a restaurant. The flesh tasted strongly of iodine, so the carcass was returned to the sea. But the photographs, horny parrot-like beak (too large to fit in a cup) and thumb-sized suckers allowed identification.

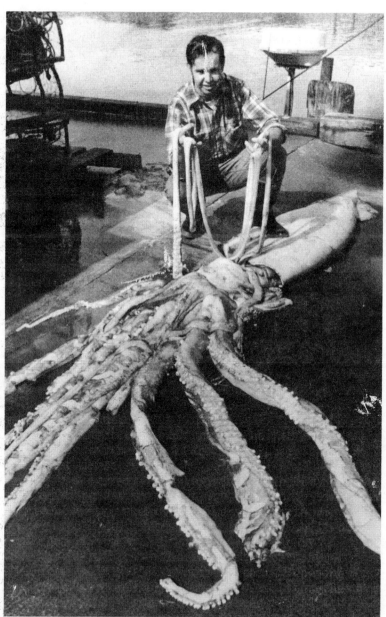

GIANT SQUID: Gary Steffensmier with only giant squid
ever caught alive in the Pacific north of Chile; off
Mack Arch, Oregon (Curry Coastal Pilot)

17. NUDIBRANCH: Two of the largest nudibranchs (sea slugs) in the world inhabit Pacific Northwest waters. Our waters are awash in nudibranchs, both in great numbers and in individual species.

As a group, nudibranchs are highly diverse in shape and color. Most are beautiful creatures, small and delicate, lacking true molluscan gills. They breathe through a variety of branched or plumed projections along the back and side. Their beauty of form is enhanced by the most brilliant colors of any marine invertebrates. The body and its projections are often tranlucent and colored, or edged or tipped with lemon yellow, pale blue, red, gold and violet.

One giant is the broad, one-foot-long "orange peel" nudibranch (Tochuina tetraquetra), orange with short, white cerata (gills) fringing an oblong body covered with knobby growths.

Our other giant is the beautiful "rainbow nudibranch" (Dendronotus iris), one foot long and 3" wide. Along its back are two rows of pointed cerata, tipped with white or purple.

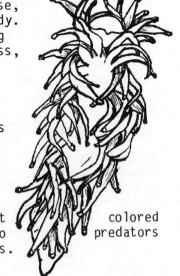

This nudibranch, one of a few able to swim, moves by folding the edges of its foot together lengthwise, and gracefully flexing its body. Other nudibranchs crawl, using their muscular foot on eelgrass, tidepool rocks or seaweed.

Not totally defenseless, larger nudibranchs eat sea anemones and hydroids, recycling their stinging cells into their own cerata. Others that live on specific hosts, often a sponge on which they also feed, have a body color matching the host's; their egg coils also match. Bright ones are often unpalatable to colored predators because of unsavory secretions.

18. SWAN: The Northwest provides winter homes for North America's largest aquatic bird, the trumpeter swan (<u>Olor buccinator</u>). This rare bird with white plumage and black bill and feet is the larger of two swans native to North America. Its largest wild (not human-fed) wintering groups in North America are in the Northwest.

This largest of the swans, one of the world's largest flying birds, measures nearly 5' long and weighs up to 35 pounds, near the upper weight limit for flying birds. Although the swans are strong fliers with an 8-foot wingspan, the heavy birds have trouble taking off and maneuvering in the air. They land on water to cushion the shock.

The trumpeters are noted for their low-pitched horn-like trumpeting. The memorable two-note whoop is usually heard in defense of territory.

Because each breeding pair requires some 30 isolated acres, nesting trumpeters are rare in the lower 48. Once, the swans were seen by the thousands over central and western North America, but early settlers shot them for skins and meat. As the isolated habitat they require was lost, the survivors migrated west and to Canada. Protected now, they are no longer an endangered species.

Washington attracts between 400 and 900 wild wintering swans; some 350 to 450 gather on Skagit County's Barney, Clear and Beaver Lakes.

In Idaho 350 to 450 gather at Henry's Fork.

19. LAND MAMMAL: The largest land mammal of the Northwest coast is the Roosevelt elk (Cervus can-adensus), a deer, not a true elk. The largest surviving population of these elk in the U.S. is on the Olympic Peninsula. More than 5000 roam Olympic National Park, traveling in small bands of 10 to 100; 10,000 others live outside the Park. Many elk summer in subalpine meadows and winter at lower altitudes, sometimes showing up on isolated Olympic National Park beaches.

The Olympic Peninsula population is fairly stable, controlled by cougars and harsh winters with deep snow. Some 30,000 others are scattered throughout western Washington. Unmistakable signs of elk presence are neatly pruned four-foot-high shrubs normally growing 15 feet high. The Hoh Rain Forest is an ideal place to see such pruning. Elk are often seen near the river there.

Larger than the more numerous Rocky Mountain elk, these bulls measure 5 to 5½ feet at the shoulder, and weigh 800 to 1000 pounds. Better proportioned than Rocky Mountain elk, they have longer legs and a more graceful body. Roosevelt elk have a richer reddish-brown coat; both males and females often display a striking black mane.

Their survival has been aided by the fact that their many-tined antlers make less desirable trophies than those of Rocky Mountain elk. They are more rugged with less length and spread.

Once common throughout the coast range down to San Francisco Bay, many were killed only for the two large upper canine teeth, much in demand as charms for a fraternal order.

One of the largest wintering populations in western Oregon, more than 200, gathers in 1200-acre Jewell Meadows Wildlife Area east of Astoria. After a successful transplanting program, this elk is increasing in numbers in Oregon.

During fall rutting season, male elk of all species bugle, making an high-pitched, unforgettable whistling sound.

20. STURGEON: The lower Columbia River probably has the world's largest and healthiest wild population of white sturgeon (<u>Acipenser transmontanus</u>). It is North America's largest sturgeon species, one of the world's three largest, and the biggest fresh-water stream-ascending fish of North American coastal waters. A primitive fish more ancient than dinosaurs, a survivor of prehistoric armored fish, today's sturgeon are larger than any prehistoric fish known.

In the Pacific Northwest white sturgeon are found in the Columbia, Umpqua, Rogue, Willamette, Snake and Kootenai; in Puget Sound, Lake Washington, Willapa Bay, and Grays Harbor. Once, Columbia River sturgeon were killed by salmon fishermen for damaging fishwheels, setlines and salmon nets (torn by the knobby skin). Once they were burned or used for fertilizer. Later, tons of sturgeon were caught on "Chinese lines" with 200 to 400 hooks, and shipped East in iced railroad cars.

Now the big fish are protected by size limits (3 to 6 feet), closure of some areas, a limit of one fish a year, or by catch-and-release laws.

White sturgeon may live more than 100 years. All species have bony head plates and bony shields on the body, yet they lack internal bones; the flexible notochord "backbone" is of cartilage.

These toothless bottom browsers (with underslung mouth that extends to suck up fish and other food) are slow growing, slow feeding, usually slow moving. A hooked sturgeon can leap a foot high.

The largest white sturgeon caught in the Pacific Northwest was 20 feet long and 1500 lbs., hooked in 1898 in Idaho's Snake River near the Weiser River. The largest recorded Columbia River white sturgeon was 12½ feet and 1285 lbs., including 125 pounds of eggs. Record fish are always females; a 50-year-old female may carry four million eggs weighing several hundred pounds.

THE FASTEST

1. ANTELOPE: The world's fastest land animal over a sustained distance is the pronghorn antelope (Antilocapra americana). A true native of North America, and found only here, it can outrun the cheetah over distances of 1000 yards or more. Aided by large heart and lungs, and padded hooves that protect against rocky ground, it can accelerate almost instantly, maintain 60 mph for half a mile, and reach 70 mph.

It is the world's only true horned animal to shed yearly from the bony core an outer sheath of black, fused hair-like keratin. The shape of the short, heavy horns is unique, branching and curving backward with the prong projecting forward.

This antelope has no near relatives. Only 3' high at the shoulder, a male may weigh 125 pounds.

For protection from wolf, golden eagle and coyote, the antelope depends upon speed, hearing and keen eyesight. Its large, heavily lashed eyes are eight times as sharp as human eyes.

Muscles in the skin move hollow, insulated hairs of the coarse coat up for cooling, down for minus-zero protection. To warn the herd of danger, each raises 3"-long white hairs on a rump rosette visible for miles. The herd always flees single-file. Once numbering perhaps 40 million, by the early 1900s they were almost exterminated. Protected now, two of the largest  Northwest herds roam Hart Mountain Antelope Refuge and four valleys in Idaho's Lemhi Mountains.

2. CLAM: The Pacific Northwest's fastest-moving clam is the razor clam (Siliqua patula), found in abundance only on beaches in southern Washington and northern Oregon. The relatively long life of the razor clam-- a legal 4½" clam for diggers is 3½ years old-- means slow recovery from winter storms, from overharvesting, and, it was thought, from the gill infection by a parasite never known before in the animal kingdom.

During the winter of 1983-1984, razor clams in Washington suffered "the single most disastrous drop in a population of animals ever heard of in so brief a period"-- up to 80% and 90%.

And yet, because of a rapid recovery, limited seasons of clamming were allowed in late 1985 and 1986, although the parasite, which attacks gill tissue, suffocating the clams, was still present.

With a thin, narrow shell up to six inches long, shaped like a straight razor, the clam can bury itself in very wet sand one inch a second, in about 8 or 9 movements of its foot. The pointed muscular foot, extended half the length of the shell, digs into the sand, then swells up, using body fluids. Next, the foot muscle, securely anchored, contracts by expelling the water, leaving a hole into which the clam is pulled. This procedure is repeated until the clam is 12 to 18 inches deep. Extended, the foot can cling so firmly to sand that sometimes the shell will be pulled off before the muscle lets go.

The ability to burrow quickly and deeply is essential on wave-washed beaches. Razor clams make no permanent burrows because they must feed near the surface on suspended organisms washed in and out by the waves. Sandy beaches, constantly built and undercut by waves, are scarce in food and security, a much harsher environment than rocky shores, and home to far fewer animals than tidepools.

THE HARSHEST HABITAT

WORM: No other animal as large as the tiny seg-
mented ice worm (<u>Mesenchytraeus solifuga</u>) lives
in such a harsh habitat: glacial ice. They are no
hoax. Ice worms were discovered in 1887 on Alaska's Muir Glacier. Possibly relics of the Ice Age,
the worms, 2/5 to 1 1/5 inch long, are found only
in coastal Pacific Northwest glaciers, from Alaska to Mount Rainier. 15 Washington glaciers have
the year-round temperature of 32° F required by
ice worms. During the day the worms descend into
the ice or into its snow cover. Winters they
spend deep in snow-insulated ice. Less hardy but
related worms live in snow, meltwater and moss
adjacent to snow, but never in ice.

The worm's optimum temperature, 32° F., is
several degrees below the "biological zero" of
most animals-- the point at which body functions
cease. Even the warmth of a human hand makes ice
worms disintegrate. Except for a diurnal species
found only on Mount Rainier, the worms, which have
not been extensively studied, shun not only sun
but even bright moonlight. Ascending to the
surface to feed, they are far more numerous on
cloudy nights. As many as 500 a square meter may
crowd together, sometimes in loose clusters with
free ends waving.

They can slither through ice so hard an ice
axe is needed to cut it. But glacial ice has
relatively large ice crystals, and the worms, lub-
ricated by a film of water, probably move along
irregularities where ice crystals melt.

Much of their food is washed from the surface
of the ice into meltwater furrows, in which they
gather. They ingest red algae, bacteria, diatoms,
pollen grains, snow fleas, protozoa, fern spores,
and minerals from air-borne dirt. In turn, they
provide food for birds; the rosy finch often feeds
on high altitude snowfields.

THE MOST ENDANGERED

CARIBOU: The most endangered, and the rarest of all U.S. land mammals is the woodland-caribou (Rangifer tarandus caribou). The last herd in the lower 48 of this subspecies of the American tundra caribou is very small-- about 30 with few of breeding age. Interbreeding has so weakened the herd that only three calves were born in 1983.

Only in the 1950s was the herd, numbering 100, discovered. Not until 1983, after pressure from Idaho's Fish and Game Department and the National Audubon Society, was the woodland-caribou protected as an endangered animal-- almost too late for the survival of the herd.

The very mobile herd primarily roams northern Idaho and the northeastern corner of Washington in the wild Selkirk Range. They live in densely forested, glaciated valleys above 4000 feet. Their splayed six-inch-wide hoofs support them on summer mud in glacial basins and on snow that may reach 50 feet deep. The snow-pack helps them reach hanging lichens, their preferred food, growing high in trees. Their long legs also help in deep snow.

Once plentiful all along the northern border, many were killed in the 1800s by trappers and packers for meat. Logging has destroyed much of the old-growth conifer forest they require. It brought roads, which brought poachers and trucks, both of which kill. And the cleared lands brought white-tailed deer, which carried a parasite fatal to many caribou. Only in mountains too wild and high for deer did a few caribou survive.

A program is now underway to resettle woodland-caribou from British Columbia in isolated areas of Idaho which provide food, cover and calving grounds.

THE ONLY

1. FROG: One of only two tailed frog families in the world (<u>Ascaphus truei</u>), the only U.S. tailed frog, lives in the Pacific Northwest in the Coast Range, Blue Mountains, Cascades and Idaho Rockies.

The tailed frogs have the oldest lineage of any frogs in the world. Their fossils are found in rocks 135 to 190 million years old. The skeleton of the very primitive, 2-inch-long frog bears a strong resemblance to that of a salamander.

The tiny frog, with unwebbed fingers and only partly webbed toes, is highly adapted for life in small, swift, noisy streams. Both male and female lack eardrums, and the male is unusual among frogs in being voiceless. The tailed frogs are usually found in mountains at 6500 feet or higher, but also in cold, coastal streams at sea level.

They prefer water barely above freezing in winter and around 50° F. in summer. Nocturnal and solitary, they spend most of the day under river rocks, emerging at night to feed on insects. In summer they move to streams with more flow.

The boneless tail, most prominent in the male, is more an extension of skin than a true tail. It has two wagging muscles, like those in a salamander tail. It is used for excretion and also for internal fertilization, essential in fast water.

The two-inch-long female, whose ¼-inch eggs are the largest of any of our native frogs, uses her less-visible tail to deposit her string of eggs under river rocks. The tadpoles have a unique sucker mouth, used for clinging to stream rocks from which they rasp algae. The tailed frog is the only frog with ribs, some of which are attached to vertebrae. These allow it, unlike other frogs, to pump air in and out.

2. WHALE STRANDING: The only mass stranding of sperm whales (<u>Physeter macrocephalus</u>) ever known in the western U.S. occurred in June 1979 on a beach at Florence, Oregon. That stranding of 41 of the world's largest toothed whales was only the second in North America and the fourth largest of 17 such strandings recorded worldwide since 1617.

Since the 12-ton whales were still alive when discovered, there was time to test tissues and blood before death and decomposition. But still, the exact cause of the stranding is not known. Their organs of echolocation were found free of ear parasites that disturb balance.

Single strandings of sick or dying whales are much more common than mass strandings, which are most often seen in the deep-water, gregarious whales with highly developed social behavior. The group may stay with sick, injured or dying members who head for shore. Spectators at Florence tried to tow some of the whales back to sea, but the whales returned to the beach.

Unused to shallow water, the whales may be unable to get good echoes from a beach like the one at Florence-- long, sloping and shallow, with no physical formations to bounce back sound.

Perhaps the whales, driven by hunger (their stomachs were empty except for squid beaks), followed a school of smaller spawning squid too close to shore. Or they might have been fleeing killer whales, a predator feared by all the great whales.

Another rare stranding occurred in February 1986 at Lincoln City, Oregon. A 15'-long Stejnegar's beaked whale was found dead on the beach, one of only 30 ever found. It was the second stranding of a beaked whale on the Oregon Coast, but never before has an intact skeleton of an adult male been found. It was the first ever discovered with a full stomach-- thousands of squid. These should tell how deep the whale dives. The rare whales, with a dolphin-like head, have two spade-shaped teeth in the lower jaw.

3   OSPREY: The osprey (Pandion haliaetus) is the only bird of prey that dives into the water after live fish, and the only one with a reversible toe that helps secure its catch. Although world-wide, ospreys belong to only one species. The handsome, two-foot-long bird with white underside and dark back is easily identified by its white neck and heavy, black cheek band.

Oregon has perhaps the Pacific Northwest's largest nesting population of ospreys in Deschutes National Forest at Crane Prairie Reservoir Osprey Management Area. A 1969 census found that most of Oregon's 48 pairs of nesting ospreys were at Crane Prairie. The reservoir that was formed by a dam flooding Crane Prairie in 1923 killed a lodge-pole pine forest. The snags and the abundance of fish were ideal for nesting ospreys. In Idaho, annual flooding where the St. Joe River flows into Lake Coeur d'Alene also killed many large trees, now used by a large population of nesting ospreys.

The ospreys, with long, sharp, curved talons and short, strong legs, are well adapted for taking slippery prey. Also helpful are the reversible toe and spiny knobs on the bottom of the foot. The sharp-eyed bird seldom misses, plummeting, feet first, wings folded, more than 100 feet. Often it hits the water forcibly enough to submerge briefly. As it flies off with a fish in its talons, a bald eagle may harass the osprey into dropping its catch, which the eagle snatches in midair. In turn,   ospreys fiercely guard their nest against bald eagles, their only natural enemy. The bulky, 2-foot-deep stick nest, added to year after year, can reach 5 feet across. Osprey eggs, slate-gray with rusty spots, are among the handsomest of bird eggs.

3. SEA LION: The only Steller's (northern) sea lions (<u>Eumetopias jubata</u>) that breed on the Pacific Northwest mainland belong to a herd of some 200 that live in a huge natural sea cave on the Oregon coast near Florence. These largest of the eared seals and largest of American sea lions normally breed offshore, many on Oregon's islands and rocks. But this herd mates and rears its pups in the Sea Lion Caves.

The male, which develops a thick mane, may be 13 feet long and weigh a ton or more. Much of the weight is body fat. It provides water and food during the two-month breeding season when the bull is so busy defending his 20 to 30 cows and his rock-ledge territory outside the caves that he seldom leaves the rookery. Dominant males protect their harems by threat displays to weaker males: biting, neck-fencing, roaring and hissing.

STELLER'S SEA LIONS with harem: largest American sea lion, only one to breed on Pacific Northwest mainland (Sea Lion Caves Inc.)

Females have little loyalty to their harem-master.

Cave bulls winter in Alaska, returning to the Caves for spring mating. During rough weather, most members stay in the huge cave, but on sunny days they swim or lounge on rocky ledges nearby.

Although these sea lions do not breed in Washington, several hundred winter in Puget Sound.

Steller's sea lions, noted for their roar, differ from true seals in being able to rotate their long hindlimbs forward, so that on land their body is raised and they can "gallop" rather rapidly for a short distance. In swimming they use the forelimbs much more than the hindlimbs.

THE MOST ELUSIVE

1. LYNX: One of the most elusive of Pacific Northwest mammals is the Canada lynx (<u>Lynx canadensis</u>). This solitary, nocturnal relative of the bobcat lives in high, remote areas forested with lodgepole pines. Okanogan National Forest in northeastern Washington has the largest Canada lynx population in the lower 48. Seldom seen, it gives away its presence by huge tracks with long strides. Thick pads of fur on the feet insulate and support the lynx on snow, helping it pursue its essential prey, the snowshoe rabbit. Agile in trees and on logs, able to leap great distances, the Canada lynx is awkward on open ground.

This cat is distinctive for its tufted ears, long ruffs sweeping down the cheeks, and stubby tail, tipped with black. The tawny or grizzled gray pelt with long silky hairs has soft, dense fur.

Despite horrible screams while fighting, this lynx is evidently more verbal than aggressive. Its pelts bear relatively few scars.

2. COUGAR: Notably shy even for a wild creature, the graceful, powerful cougar (<u>Felis concolor</u>) is one of the two most elusive carnivores of the Pacific Northwest. Also known as mountain lion, puma and panther, the tawny-coated cougar is the second largest New World cat, largest of three native Pacific Northwest cats. Males may be 8 feet long plus 30 inches of tail. Large ones can weigh more than 150 pounds.

Seldom seen even by veteran outdoorsmen, they prefer dense cover in rugged terrain, near big-game species such as deer or elk, which they kill by a leap to the back, breaking the neck or biting the throat. They can leap 30 feet on level ground.

Their presence is known by their large tracks, made by padded paws 7 inches across; by remains of a kill, often grass- or dirt-covered; by scratch marks on trees; and by territorial piles of scat.

Cougars mew, whistle, hiss, spit, growl and purr. Prolonged, spine-tingling screams may come from mating females or from males signaling a mate or defying another male. Males will kill and eat other male cougars.

Unless starving, cougars usually avoid humans and their buildings. But they are very curious, watching humans for hours, even stalking hunters.

In the 1700s cougars had the widest range of any New World cat, in every state of the lower 48, and coast to coast from British Columbia to South America. Now, these secretive, solitary cats are found mainly in the West in small groups. All 3 Pacific Northwest states have mountain wilderness areas and ample deer and elk that cougars require.

Washington may have the most cougars in the Pacific Northwest, perhaps 2000, concentrated in the Olympics, Selkirks and Okanogan country. Oregon and Idaho have some 1500 each. Populations remain rather stable and well spaced because of a low birth rate and huge territorial requirements, estimated at up to 100 square miles for males. They seldom leave their territory unless starving.

THE FIERCEST PREDATOR

WHALE: Gentle with humans, compassionate with its own kind, highly social, intelligent, playful, articulate, the killer whale (Orcinus orca) is the sea's fiercest predator, with no natural enemies. Largest of the true dolphins, orcas can be 25 feet long and weigh 8 to 10 tons.

Voracious and sharp-toothed, they are the only cetacean to eat other cetaceans, and the fastest of marine mammals that prey on other marine mammals. Capable of brief spurts at 34 mph, they are one of the fastest creatures in the sea.

In the open ocean, unlike most whales, orcas travel in precisely ordered packs, side by side, and attack whales many times their size. A pack of 30 orcas was filmed attacking a young 60-foot blue whale, largest animal alive at 100 feet and 150 tons. Efficiently they divided up the labor: herding on both sides, and above and below to prevent escape, trying to cover the blowhole.

After crippling the whale by chewing off the dorsal fin and shredding the tail flukes, the orcas stripped away chunks of flesh and blubber. Often they chew a whale's lips, force their snout into its mouth, and tear out the tongue.

Puget Sound has three resident pods of orcas which feed mainly on salmon, almost never on other sea mammals. Only transient orcas eat Puget Sound harbor seals and sea lions. The permanent pods are designated J, K and L, with each member identified by unique markings and given a number. They cruise the Strait of Juan de Fuca, British Columbia inland waters and Puget Sound on a quite predictable course, often logging 100 miles a day. Those 79 whales are one of the world's most accessible and largest concentrations of orcas. The most frequently sighted orcas in the U.S., they are also the world's most intensively studied whales.

In summer they swim regularly, about every

three days, along the southwest coast of San Juan Island, where Lime Kiln Park was created in August 1984. This is the nation's first and only park for whale-watching and research, one of the few places in the U.S. where scientists can study the same orcas year-round.

Each of the three pods has its distinctive language of clicks, grunts and whistles. Though each is a family group, the pods travel and hunt together, and interbreed.

THE DENSEST POPULATION

1. MARINE LIFE: Nowhere else in the world do marine animals grow in such abundance and diversity as in Pacific Northwest waters, especially in Puget Sound and the Strait of Juan de Fuca. 2000 different kinds of invertebrates thrive there. Washington's irregular coastline provides a variety of habitats: rocky shores, tide pools, quiet bays, estuaries, sandy beaches. Nutrients come from river run-off and from tidal currents which stir up from ocean bottom sediments, cold deep water rich in decaying plant and animal matter.

A complex of marine laboratories was located near Friday Harbor on San Juan Island by the University of Washington Zoology Department, rated second in the U.S. by the National Academy of Science. The site was chosen for its varied marine life and habitats, and a variety of depths, salinity, and sea floor made accessible by 12-foot tides. Each summer 100 researchers come to study marine animals in their natural habitat. Important neurological research done there on invertebrates has proved to have valuable human applications.

2. BADGER: The densest concentration of badgers
(Taxidea taxus neglecta) in North America is
found in Idaho's Snake River Birds of Prey Natural
Area. Some 15 a square mile compete with raptors
for the many rodents, rabbits, and reptiles.

These fierce, heavy-bodied and squat members
of the weasel family are powerful excavators.
With strong short legs and heavy front claws, they
can disappear into the ground in seconds. They
have no permanent burrows. When they need to rest
or sleep, they quickly dig another burrow. The
many holes are dangerous for stock and horses.

In the Pacific Northwest badgers are found in
grasslands and sagebrush areas east of the Cascades. Nocturnal and solitary, they are seldom
seen above ground in daylight. Few animals, even
dogs, are a match for badgers.

During the longest badger trek recorded, in
1983 an ear-tagged yearling
female traveled some 60 miles
from the Idaho Birds of Prey
area over rugged moun-
tains, badlands and
across the Snake River
to Oregon's Malheur
County. Many adult
badgers never move from one small area.

3. BIRDS OF PREY: North America's densest concentration of nesting birds of prey, some 600
pairs of 14 species, is found in Idaho's 32,000-
acre Snake River Birds of Prey Natural Area. The
area is unique, perhaps in the world, for the number and variety of birds of prey that nest there:
eagles, hawks, falcons, owls, ospreys, vultures.

In some areas along a 33-mile stretch of rugged river canyon in the desert, basalt nesting
cliffs rise more than 500 feet above the river,
providing thermals on which the raptors soar.
Each year more nesting raptors are attracted to

the area with its rocky ledges and pinnacles than
to any other North American area of similar size.

The food supply is abundant: snakes, lizards,
jackrabbits, rodents such as kangaroo rats and
deer mice, and Townsend ground squirrels.

Golden eagles and great horned owls are year-
round residents. Migratory raptors include red-
tailed and ferruginous hawks, and prairie falcons.
Among wintering raptors are American kestrels,
rough-legged hawks and a few bald eagles.

The World Center for Birds of Prey was established in 1984 with the Peregrine Fund's entire
captive breeding population of the endangered fal-
con: 119. Peregrines are the fastest, most skilled
of all flyers, diving at nearly 200 mph. Their
sharp eyes can see a pigeon at 3500'.

*BALD EAGLE harassing OSPREY (painting by Richard Amundsen;
photo by Saling)*

4. SQUID: The densest population of larger marine animals in Pacific Northwest waters, as elsewhere in the world, is made up of smaller squid of
various species. Potential harvests have been estimated at 100 million tons. Schools of smaller
squid are so immense that they give false bottom
readings to ships. Spawning squid form incredi-
bly extensive surface layers; one ship sailed for
two hours through an unbroken carpet of squid extending in all directions to the horizon.

Squid are ancient animals, cephalopods,-- the
most highly developed and organized invertebrates
and mollusks. The largest of all invertebrates is
the giant squid, which has the biggest eye of any
living creature, more than 15" in diameter. That
complex "camera" eye is better in some ways than
the human eye, its retina more finely structured.

Torpedo-shaped and jet-propelled, the squid is
the fastest invertebrate in the sea over a short
distance, and one of the deadliest of predators.
As vicious as it is voracious, it will kill when
not hungry. A powerful parrot-like beak centered
within its arms bites its prey in the neck.

Along with the octopus it has the largest invertebrate brain, protected in a cartilage case.
Some luminescent species are the most spectacularly beautiful of all invertebrates, with the most
highly developed light-producing organs known.
Light cells glowing with color can stud many parts
of the body, even ringing the eyes.

The squid's high-pressure blood system is
unique among invertebrates, fully enclosed, with
veins and arteries, and two auxiliary hearts to
provide the extra oxygen its speed demands. The
largest nerve fibers in the animal world, used in
neural research, are found in squid, which have
the most highly developed central nervous system
of all invertebrates. Its nervous energy makes
the squid almost impossible to keep captive. Squid
can easily smother in the ink they spurt out when
disturbed. They can leap out of aquarium tanks.

5. SEABIRDS: The densest nesting colonies in the lower 48 of rhinocerous auklet (Cerorhinca monocerata), and the world's fourth largest breeding colony of that bird are found on Washington's Protection Island, 1½ miles off the mouth of Discovery Bay near Port Townsend. One-third of North America's rhinocerous auklets breed in Washington, more than half of them on Protection Island-- some 17,000 nesting pairs.

The island, saved from threatened development by the creation there of a national wildlife refuge in 1982, is the most important seabird nesting area in Washington inland waters, perhaps in the Pacific Northwest. There are no ground predators to molest eggs. Two-thirds of the seabirds that breed in Puget Sound nest there, including the state's largest glaucous-winged gull colony (4300 pairs), and 64% of its tufted puffins.

The rhinocerous auklet, dark, chunky and crow-sized, has a short "horn" atop its yellowish beak, which it uses along with clawed feet to dig its burrow. Seldom seen, the birds fish by day and stay in their burrow at night. After dusk both male and female auklets work constantly and noisily on their nesting burrows. Dug 3 to 10' into steep sandy cliffs, burrows are used for years. The birds require easily dug soil and high, unobstructed slopes that aid take-off. The stubby-winged auklets drop many feet before becoming airborne. Returning at dusk, with small fish such as herring dangling from their beak, they may awkwardly crash-land.

Far more at home underwater, auklets enter the water head-first, tipping over like ducks, but with wings open. They swim rapidly not far under the surface, webbed feet steering.

6. WATERFOWL: The densest and most spectacular concentrations of migrating waterfowl and shorebirds in North America, and perhaps in the world, are found in the Pacific Northwest. Many of the 26 national wildlife refuges (NWR) in the Pacific Northwest were created primarily for migrating birds. Many hundreds of thousands of waterfowl migrating along the various corridors of the Pacific Flyway stop to rest and feed twice a year in such Washington areas as Grays Harbor, Bowerman Basin, Willapa Bay and Willapa NWR, Padilla Bay National Estuarine Sanctuary, Dungess NWR, the San Juan Islands, and Skagit Flats WRA. In Oregon, migrating birds stop at seven refuges in addition to the spectacular concentrations at Klamath Forest, Upper and Lower Klamath, and Malheur NWRs.

The areas are critical to birds flying from as far away as Peru, and making a feeding and resting stop before the last 1500 miles to the Arctic.

Different species arrive at different times. They include western sandpipers (85% of the total) coots, black turnstones, Canada and snow geese, harlequin and other ducks, red-throated and arctic loon, phalaropes, dunlin, plover, whimbrels and black brant. Permanent or wintering residents include: hawks, pelicans, owls, great blue herons, egrets, grebes, golden and bald eagles.

Many thousands of migrating birds also rest and feed in Idaho, which has four corridors of the Pacific Flyway crossing it, and six NWRs.

Willapa Bay, whose 10,000 acres of lagoons and salt marshes and a protected island in its southwest corner attract thousands of migrating birds, is the last, large unspoiled estuary in the U.S. At low tide almost a mile of mud is exposed, providing hours of feeding for the birds.

A large part of the world's population of western sandpipers stops at Bowerman Basin (Grays Harbor). The birds feed in the mudflats on a small amphipod which is concentrated as densely as 55,000 a square meter.

THE MOST RESTRICTED HABITAT

1. DEER: The Columbian white-tailed deer (Odo-
coileus virginianus leucurus) has the most restricted habitat of any of North America's three
dozen white-tailed deer subspecies. One of only
two endangered white-tails, it is found only in
Pacific Northwest sloughs, marshes, meadows and
floodplains along the lower Columbia River and
near Roseburg, Oregon. Once abundant west of the
Cascades in Oregon's Willamette and Umpqua Valleys
and along the lower Columbia north to Puget Sound,
they were seen in quantity by Lewis and Clark. But
the deer lost its brushy habitat as settlers
cleared the land. Concentrated along rivers and
streams, they were more vulnerable to hunters.
    By 1930 the deer were believed to be extinct,
but in the late 1930s a small herd was discovered
near the Columbia River. Evidently the deer had
survived because they are smaller and can forage
under cover that discourages other deer.
    In 1972 the 4800-acre Columbian White-tailed
Deer National Wildlife Refuge was established on 3
Columbia River islands and part of the mainland.
Nearly 250 of the rare deer are now protected
there. They can often be seen on Puget Island.
    White-tailed deer are distinctive in having
broad triangular tails, brown
above and white below. When
alarmed, the deer flip up the
tail to flash a white warning
to other members of the group.
Interestingly, if a deer believes
it has not been seen, it may
keep the tail down and try
to slip away. The antlers
of these deer are unusual
in having prongs growing
from a single beam
instead of a two-forked beam.

2.   **MARMOT:** The Olympic marmot (<u>Marmota Olympus</u>) is found only in the high country of Olympic National Park, and it is the only marmot species in the Olympic Mountains. Its main burrow usually is located under single boulders or trees, or on open talus slopes. Other burrows used for escape from predators, mainly golden eagles, are dug in the feeding meadows.

This marmot is unique among all marmots in undergoing a dark molt before hibernation. When the Olympic marmot leaves its burrow in spring, its coat is golden-brown, but in late summer, the fur begins to darken.

Very social, the Olympic marmot adults often live in colonies with their young, of whom they are quite tolerant. Each morning the marmots go from burrow to burrow, greeting colony members. The yearlings may be allowed to stay with the colony when winter-kill in the burrows has been high, and fewer members will be feeding in the same meadow. The kill results when snow, which insulates the burrows, melts unseasonally, allowing cold to penetrate into the burrow. The young, with less fat stored, are most vulnerable.

Several colonies often share a feeding meadow. This tolerance may be the result of the harsh environment. In only a few summer weeks enough body fat -- up to half the body weight -- must be accumulated to last the nine months of hibernation.

All marmots are true hibernators; they do not cache food for winter. As they lie curled in the burrows, body temperature drops to near-ambient, blood pressure falls, the brain partly closes down its activity, and the heart slows to four beats a minute from its usual four a second. Yet in the spring only two hours is needed for recovery.

The Olympic marmot may be an offshoot -- isolated by the Ice Age -- of an original North American alpine form of the larger hoary marmot, largest of North American marmots, found farther east in the Cascades up to 8000 feet.

3. FISH: As a result of isolation in pockets,
often small, that survived ice age encroachment,
some rare fish that live nowhere else in the world
live in extremely restricted habitats in the Pacific Northwest. The endangered Borax Lake Chub
lives only in Oregon's unusual Borax Lake, now a
protected preserve. The ten-acre lake is isolated
in arid country and fed by thermal springs that
warm the water. Since the lake doesn't freeze in
winter, many birds nest there.

The Klamath Lake sculpin lives only above
Klamath Falls; the Alvord chub, only in a desert
basin lake below Steens Mountain; and the Warner
sucker, only in small lakes below Hart Mountain.

Idaho's Wood River sculpin, found in only one
other U.S. stream system, is protected in the
Stapp-Soldier Creek Preserve, established in 1983
in Camas County. Bear Lake on the Idaho-Utah border is home to four prehistoric native fish isolated there for millions of years and found nowhere
else: Cisco, Bear Lake and Bonneville whitefish,
and the Bear Lake sculpin. Bear Lake, 21 miles
long, 8 miles wide and 200 feet deep, is the
largest freshwater remnant of huge ancient Lake
Bonneville, which once covered most of southeastern Idaho and northern Utah.

The Olympic mudminnow (Novumbra hubbsi
Schultz), 2 to 3 inches long, was probably once
widespread; its fossils are found in Oregon. Now
it lives only in quiet water in coastal Olympic
Peninsula bogs, swamps, and marshy streams.

A courting mudminnow male expands its brightly
colored fins and moves its body strongly from side
to side. Males stalk prey and warn intruders by a
threat display. As it moves very slowly toward
the intruder, the body stiffens, fins expand and
vibrate. Then it strikes quickly and repeatedly
with its head or body. When meeting other males
at territory boundaries, mudminnows expand mem-
branes that double the head size. The territory
each so fiercely protects is only 1.7" by 3.4".

THE MOST BEAUTIFUL

HERON: History confirms that our great blue
heron (Ardes herodius fannini) has the most
beautiful breeding plumage of any Pacific Northwest bird, with colors more striking than those of
the egret. Both herons and egret males were once
killed for their breeding plumes, much in demand
for women's hats. Their slaughter caused protests
and Congress, responding to the first great U.S.
conservation movement, protected the two birds,
passing the 1918 Migratory Bird Treaty Act.
   The breeding plumage of the male great blue
heron is striking both in color and texture, with
subtle and beautifully arranged colors. A black
crest of plumes sweeps back over the head, and
longer white plumes gracefully adorn the lower
throat and breast. Plumage on the back is a lovely slate-blue. During courtship the plumes are
held erect as the head stretches high.
   Herons lack oil glands to keep their feathers
water-repellent. Instead, they preen with a powder from special areas of fine filaments that
crumble when rubbed with the bill. Using a flattened and serrated claw, the heron combs out the
powder, which rids contour feathers of eel-slime.
   This long-billed, long-necked, long-legged
bird, which stands up to 52 inches tall, is the
second tallest wading bird of the Pacific Northwest. Only our greater sandhill crane is taller.
All legs and neck, the heron weighs a mere six to
eight pounds. Unlike cranes, flying herons double
the neck back against the shoulders in an S.
   The heron builds its nest 40 to 100 feet high
in trees or snags. A single tree may hold 100
nests, each more than 2 feet deep and 3 feet in
diameter. Added to year after year, the poorly
built stick nests become so heavy they can topple
during a storm. The rather timid heron is solitary except when breeding and nesting.

THE MOST UNEXPECTED

LIFE IN VOLCANIC AREA: The most unexpected return of animal life to a ravaged area occurred at Mount St. Helens in an area so devastated by the May 1980 eruption that it was expected to be a wasteland for many years. Yet every species of animal living on pre-eruptive Mount St. Helens has been seen there since: elk, bear, deer, cougar.

Trout and salmon have spawned in rivers and streams damaged by the blast. Salmon proved surprisingly tolerant of suspended sediment. Trout survived in most of 25 larger lakes and are reproducing in two lakes a few miles from the crater.

Elk and deer herds have returned to most areas where grass has been replanted. Frogs, mice, salamanders, and snakes are back. Some small mammals, including weasels and pocket gophers, apparently survived the blast underground.

The gophers, burrowing for food and shelter, have pushed up mounds of rich soil from beneath the ash. Bodies of the many large animals that were killed also enriched the soil for plant life.

The first insects to return either fell prey to predators, or they starved, enriching the soil with their bodies. Some members of hibernating ant colonies survived, insulated from the blast. Only a few weeks after the eruption, carpenter ants were found. Fewer individuals were present but the same number of species. Even the first year, spiders were numerous in the ash.

Birds with varied diets, like mountain bluebirds and dark-eyed juncos, returned. Those with specialized diets did not. With no living trees for bark beetles, woodpeckers are absent.

Bacteria found on the rock dome in the crater, where temperatures reached 212° F., support a theory that the first living microorganisms were produced when submarine volcanic hot springs reacted with minerals and metals in the ocean.

PART TWO

THE PLANT WORLD

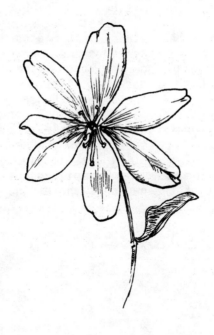

THE MOST USEFUL

1. TREE: The most useful native plant to the Pacific Northwest coastal Indians was the western redcedar tree (<u>Thuja plicata</u>). From the easily split boards they made posts, roofboards, house planks. The hollowed-out trunk provided material for dugout canoes. Sixty-foot-long war canoes could carry 30 to 40 warriors or tons of freight.

Shredded cedar bark was used for towels, diapers and cradle padding, and for tinder for fire and long-burning torches. The bark was used for skirts, fishnets, baskets, capes, rope, dresses; women wove bark strips into plates, platters, and matting for sails and summer houses. Coiled baskets were made from the tough, flexible roots. Indians valued cedar buds, tips and bark for medicine, and scoured the body with leaves and limbs.

Western redcedar is the most rot-resistant and aromatic conifer, and the easiest to split. Cedar trees cut by pioneers, who scorned them and left them lying, are still useful, almost rot-free after 200 years. The Olympic Peninsula still supplies most of the nation's shakes and shingles.

DUGOUT CANOE OF WESTERN REDCEDAR: Northwest Indians' most useful plant; at Makah Culture & Research Center (Saling)

2. BARK: Today, the most useful bark of a Northwest tree comes from the cascara buckthorn (<u>Rhamnus purshiana</u>). Pharmaceutical companies use several million pounds a year of the dried bark in making laxatives. Northwest Indians also used the bitter-tasting bark to make laxatives and a tonic, and for yellow and green dyes. The natural bark has not yet been replaced by synthetics.

The buds are unique in being unprotected by scales, covered only with thick brown hairs.

THE MOST FORMIDABLE

SHRUB: The most formidable shrub in the Pacific Northwest is the profusely spined devil's club (<u>Oplopanax horridum</u>). Stems and leaves are armored with 3/8-inch-long yellowish spines. Each maple-like leaf, with 7 to 9 lobes, has a forest of spines on its lower side. Leaves, sometimes a foot across, reach for the sun on stalks often ten feet high. Usually growing in moist woods near a

stream, devil's club is well known to hikers. The
thorns cause a painful swelling. Prostrate run-
ners from thickets can trip the unwary.

   Northwest coastal Indians boiled the peeled
bark and drank the infusion to cure a cold or T.B.
Shamans used the shrub in rituals for protection
against supernatural beings. A legendary hero
pursued by an enemy threw a bit of devil's club
behind him, and at once, an impenetrable thicket
of devil's club sprang up to protect him.

THE LONGEST-LIVED TREES

1. ALASKA-CEDAR: An Alaska-cedar (Chamaecyparis
nootkatensis) may live 2000 years. A tree 1000
years old may be only 100 feet high. At timberline, it may become a sprawling shrub, growing on
rocks in little or no soil. Also called yellow-
cedar, the rot-resistant tree is one of only a few
trees seldom growing east of the Cascades, preferring the moist coastal side 2500 to 6500 feet
high. One exception: a 10-acre grove in central
Oregon that is probably an Ice Age remnant. The
fine-grained wood takes a high polish.

2. WESTERN JUNIPER: Western juniper (Juniperus
occidentalis) may hold the record for Pacific
Northwest tree longevity; one growing in Utah is
about 3000 years old. Western juniper is often
the only tree that can grow in Oregon's hot, arid
High Desert country. The hardy, gnarled, little
tree can survive with an annual 8 inches of precipitation. Its northernmost limits are near Pasco in eastern Washington, where the state's largest grove, really a scattering of older trees with
few seedlings, barely survives among active sand
dunes. In 1984 the Washington Wilderness Bill
created the Juniper Dunes Wilderness.

THE MOST HIGHLY MODIFIED LEAF

CARNIVOROUS PLANT: The cobra lily (<u>Darlingtonia</u> <u>californica</u>), the only member of the carnivorous pitcher plant found in the Pacific Northwest, has the most highly modified leaf of any Northwest plant. The leaf has the most complicated structure of any pitcher plant leaf in the U.S. It is the largest and most spectacular plant carnivore in the Pacific Northwest, where four of six U.S. genera of carnivorous plants grow.

The cobra lily is one of the Northwest's most highly localized plants. It grows only in wet, acid peat or sphagnum on the southwest coast of Oregon and up to 8000 feet in the Siskiyous.

The pale-green leaf, with a reptilian "head" veined with red or purple, resembles a striking cobra. Below an opening in the dome dangles a "fishtail," a handy landing platform for insects.

The leaf, up to 3 feet tall, has become intri-
cately adapted for the capture and digestion of
insects. As it grows, it twists so that the opening in the dome faces outward, the better to catch
such insects as wasps, bees, ants, flies, beetles.
An 18-acre bog crammed with cobras forms a
Botanical Wayside exhibit a few miles north of
Florence, Oregon. Growing in nitrogen-poor soil,
the plant supplements its diet with insects, which
it lures by rich nectar glands on the leaf and
fishtail. Hairs pointing upward encourage the
insect feeding on nectar to move toward the mouth.
Clear spots on the dome seem to offer exits, but,
once inside and ready to leave, the insects tire
themselves by flying against those "windows."
Unable to walk on the slick surface against a
forest of hairs that now point downward, insects
fall into a pool of liquid secreted at the base of
the leaf. There, bacteria digest soft parts of
the body, and plant walls absorb the nutrients.

THE HARSHEST ENVIRONMENT

MOUNTAIN HEMLOCK: Although western juniper survives dry climate and poor soil, and Alaska-cedar
thrives in very wet coastal soil and stays alive
in scanty timberline soil, the mountain hemlock
(Tsuga mertensiana) endures the harshest conditions of any Pacific Northwest tree. It survives
the continent's deepest, wettest snow-- on Mount
Rainier-- along with heavy spring runoff and abundant rainfall. On timberline glacial moraines it
quickly sprouts, as well as on recent lava flows
where moisture is sufficient. It grows high on
Crater Lake's rim, and is abundant in northern Idaho's Bitterroot Mountains. At timberline it becomes gnarled, scrubby, and sprawling. In the
most unforgiving environments, it reproduces by
layering of the lower limbs.

THE MOST ELUSIVE

1. ORCHID: The most elusive and most beautiful of the Pacific Northwest's 34 orchid species is the phantom or snow orchid (Eburophyton austiniae). Never abundant and seldom seen, the rare orchid is found mainly on the Olympic Peninsula, in the Cascades of Oregon and Washington, and in west-central Idaho. It always grows in conifer forests, dense and undisturbed, with little sunshine. Those who see one never reveal its site.

Stems, flowers, and sheath-like leaves are white except for a bit of yellow in the flower throat. Stems 8 to 20 inches long bear fragrant flower spikes of 5 to 20 waxy, translucent blooms a half-inch long. Deriving nourishment from decaying vegetation, this lovely saprophyte flowers only rarely, perhaps once in 17 years. A few are protected in 40-acre Major Creek Preserve in Washington's Klickitat County.

2. KALMIOPSIS: Another very elusive, seldom-seen plant is a small rhododendron-like shrub, Kalmiopsis leachiana, a member of the heath family found in 1930. One of the rarest Pacific Northwest plants, often just 6 to 12 inches high, it grows only in a small area of southwest Oregon, up to 5000 feet high, in the rugged 180,000-acre Kalmiopsis Wilderness within Siskiyou National Forest. More than 1400 species of plants, shrubs and trees grow there, many of them rare. A few Kalmiopsis are also found near the Umpqua River.

The prehistoric plant, a pre-Ice-Age relict, roots in cracks and crevices on steep hillsides in the rain shadow of coastal mountains, and bears clusters of 3/4-inch pink blossoms that contrast strikingly with glossy, dark green leaves.

THE ONLY

1. YEW: The only common tree-like yew in North America is the Pacific yew (Taxus brevifolia), a small, slow-growing tree with strong, springy, fine-grained wood. It is unique among Pacific Northwest conifers in sending out permanent shoots from cut stumps. This durable hardwood was used by Pacific Northwest Indians for spoons, boxes, drum frames, digging sticks for clams and tubers, log-splitting wedges, clubs and harpoon shafts, bows and arrows, and canoe paddles.

2. FIRE-ADAPTED CONIFER: The only conifer whose cones have become adapted to forest fires is the inland lodgepole pine (Pinus contorta var. latifolia). It grows mainly east of the Cascades to the Rockies. Scales of the 2-inch-long, prickly cone are often sealed by resin. Only the heat of a forest fire unseals them. Able to germinate on burned soil, the tiny seeds get a headstart on other seeds. Unsealed cones on the same tree release seed normally. Often cones hang on the trees for many years, their seeds still viable even when the trunk grows over the cones.

3. DECIDUOUS CONIFER: Western larch (Larix occidentalis) is the only deciduous native conifer in the Pacific Northwest, one of only two in North America. Abundant in all three Northwest states, it is the world's largest larch. Except for sequoias, it has the largest proportion of limbless trunk in relation to its height of any North American tree. In inland Pacific Northwest, the young western larch is often the fastest growing tree, important since it is intolerant of shade. Its wood is one of the heaviest, densest and most fire-resistant of any conifer, yet splits easily.

4. RAIN FORESTS: The world's only temperate-zone coniferous rain forests peak along a 50-mile section of the Olympic Peninsula in three glaciated river valleys: the Hoh, Queets and Quinault. The Hoh Rain Forest is one of the world's largest and most impressive coniferous rain forests. The Pacific Northwest also has the most accessible virgin forest remaining in the U.S.

Rain forests exist here because of humidity, maintained by ocean fog, many cloudy days, and huge amounts of gentle rainfall (120 to 140 inches a year); several feet of rich forest soil, drained by hundreds of feet of glacially deposited gravel and rock underneath it; lush undergrowth and leaf canopies blocking sunshine from the forest floor and keeping the air cool and moist; U-shaped glacial valleys whose broad, gently sloping walls and floors minimize root soil erosion; huge fallen "nurse logs" supporting tree seedlings otherwise unable to compete with lush groundcover.

TEMPERATE RAIN FORESTS: world's largest, most accessible
(Bob & Ira Spring)

5. CAMAS: The only Pacific Northwest flowering plant over which wars were fought was the camas (Camassia quamash). The 1-inch, onion-like bulb was the Northwest Indians' most widely traded food next to dried salmon, so important that some tribes, including the Nez Perce, fought intertribal wars over favored camas meadows a mile long.

Camas grow extensively in grassy places from sea level to subalpine, both east and west of the Cascades. For centuries the Nez Perce Indians dug in Idaho's Weippe Meadow and Big Camas Prairie.

Special digging hooks of curved animal bones or pointed hardwood sticks were used. After being roasted for several days, the bulbs were sun-dried and pounded into flour. The sweetish bulbs were often boiled into a syrup.

The camas also started a war between early settlers and Indians because of settlers putting livestock on traditional Indian camas lands. One day in 1878 a band of Bannocks came to dig bulbs at Big Camas Prairie near Fairfield only to find hogs rooting up and eating the bulbs. An argument followed, and some white herders were shot. The Bannocks fought a war for their rights to the camas-digging grounds, but they lost.

In 1985 huge amounts of fire-cracked rock were found in northeastern Washington's Kalispell Valley. Carbon-dated to 2000 B.C., they were used for pit-ovens to roast camas. This is the largest, earliest, and best-preserved food processing site ever found in the Northwest interior.

Camas have narrow grassy leaves and showy, hyacinth-like clusters of two- to three-inch flowers borne on two-foot-tall stems. Flowers vary in color from iridescent pale blue to deep purplish blue. Camas meadows thick with blooms looked like "lakes of fine clear water" to Lewis and Clark.

THE MOST SHADE-TOLERANT

1. HEMLOCK: The Pacific Northwest's most shade-tolerant conifer is the western hemlock (<u>Tsuga heterophylla</u>). Really a pine, this state tree of Washington is the most abundant coastal conifer because of its tolerance for the shade of the huge trees with which it grows. Because western hemlock has the most prolific seedlings of all conifers on nurselogs, in time it tends to dominate coastal forests undisturbed by fire and logging. Its closely set branches also produce the densest shade of any conifer. Stands of old western hemlock are so dense they outproduce the larger Douglas fir in areas of similar size. Not fussy about soil or sun, the trees do require abundant rainfall.

2. FLOWERING TREE: The Pacific Northwest's most shade-tolerant flowering tree is Pacific dogwood (<u>Cornus nuttali</u>), North America's largest native dogwood, found among huge conifers in all Northwest low-elevation coastal forests. It is unique among hardwoods in preferring shade, growing among huge conifers. The white outer petals are really bracts, four to six that are sometimes five inches across. The small greenish cluster in the center is the true flower. Indians used the bark for making a laxative. 500-year-old Indian artifacts made of the very hard wood-- bows, combs, a weaver's tool-- were found perfectly preserved in the Ozette Village archeological dig. Although seldom found inland, some dogwood trees grow in northern Idaho's Lochsa River Canyon off Lewis and Clark Highway.

THE LARGEST

1. FUNGUS: The world's largest tree fungus (Oxyporus nobilissimus) was found in 1946 in Mount Rainier National Park. Measuring 56 by 37 inches, it weighed more than 300 pounds. The non-edible, woody fungus was found at the base of a western hemlock, its preferred growing site. Unusual among fungus in being perennial, it had 35 annual growth layers.

2. TREE: Largest non-Sequoia tree in the world is Douglas fir (Pseudotsuga menziesii), really a hemlock. A century ago, 300-foot-high Douglas firs were not rare. At Oregon's building at the Panama-Pacific International Exposition in 1915, a Douglas-fir flagpole nearly 300 feet high was displayed. Douglas fir is the main source of the world's lumber, noted for its strength and lightness. It is the best-adapted western tree, tolerating more different types of forest than any other species, although very intolerant of shade.

Washington has the fewest Douglas firs of the three Pacific Northwest states but the largest. Those found inland are slower growing. Oregon, whose state tree is the Douglas fir, has had two world-record Douglas firs, but each has blown down, returning the record to Washington's Queets Fir. Still unclaimed in 1986 was a reward for anyone finding in Oregon a Douglas fir larger than Washington's 1000-year-old, broken-top champion (off-again-on-again since the early 1950s).

In pioneer days these forest giants were so huge that two men needed three days to get one down. Too large for the saws available then, many were toppled by burning. First, giant augers were used to bore two holes down into the trunk. Then one hole was heaped with burning coals; the other served as a chimney.

3. TREES: Of the 13 tallest trees in the U.S., seven grow in Washington and Oregon. The three Northwest states hold world or national records for the largest individuals of many tree species, and, often, also the tallest. Washington rain forests in Olympic National Park have some of the largest-known individual trees of five species. Oregon has 56 national champions of 52 species, including: bigleaf maple 96', Sauvie Island; black cottonwood, 155', Willamette Mission State Park; Cascara buckthorn, 37' (3 Oregon specimens); Pacific dogwood, 50', Clatskanie; Port-Orford-cedar, 219', Siskiyou N.F.; Western white pine, 239', near Medford; white alder, 80', Eola, OR.

WORLD RECORD TREES

ALASKA-CEDAR: 120' high, 37'8½" circum., Olympic N.P.(Quinault), WA., 500-600 years old.

DOUGLAS FIR: 221' high, 45' 5" circum., Olympic N.P. (Queets River), WA., 1000 years old.

ENGELMANN SPRUCE: 179' high, 24' 2" circum., Payette Lake, Idaho.

GRAND FIR: 231' high, 20' 8" circum., Olympic N.P., (Barnes Creek), WA.

NOBLE FIR: 278' high, 28' 4" circum., Gifford Pinchot N.F., WA.

SITKA SPRUCE: 216' high, 52.6' circum., near Seaside, Oregon, 700 years old.

SUBALPINE FIR: 206' high, 21', 7" circum., Olympic N.P. (Bogachiel River),WA.

WESTERN HEMLOCK: 195' high, Tillamook, Oregon.

WESTERN REDCEDAR: 178' high, 61' circum., near Forks, WA, 700 to 1000 years old.

4. PLANT LEAF: The skunk cabbage (<u>Lysichitum americanum</u>) has the largest leaf of any Northwest native plant. This true Pacific Northwest native, one of the earliest spring plants, has a thin oblong leaf often more than 3 feet long and 1 foot broad. One leaf reported was 56" by 29". The huge leaves with fleshy midrib were used by Northwest Indians as berry and water containers, to make a cure-all infusion, and in cooking pits to cover and flavor camas bulbs, a staple food.

The leaves spring up from the base of the plant several weeks after the yellow spathe (hood) appears. The spathe is not a flower but a colored bract enclosing a fleshy club crowded with hundreds of small, green true flowers.

Skunk cabbage, not really malodorous, always grows where moisture is abundant, often in swampy lowlands but also in coastal forests and up to 4000 feet high in the Cascades. Despite the presence in all parts of the plant of calcium oxylate crystals, which cause an intense burning sensation and irritation of mouth and throat when the plant is eaten, Northwest Indians ate the spathe and root after steaming or roasting them for days. Dried roots were ground into flour. Heated leaves and spathes were applied to painful wounds and swellings, and to rheumatic joints.

5. TREE LEAF: The largest leaf of any Northwest native tree is that of the bigleaf maple (<u>Acer macrophyllum</u>), our only large native maple, and the largest maple species in North America. The giant leaves with five deeply cut lobes measure 8 to 12 inches across. These huge deciduous trees, which prefer the moist lowlands of western Washington and Oregon, are heavily draped with moss and lichens in rain forests. Wet epiphytes on their sturdy limbs may weigh a ton.

6. CONIFER CONES: The largest cones of a Northwest conifer, 10 to 16 inches long, grow on the sugar pine (<u>Pinus lambertiana</u>) whose northernmost limits are in southwest Oregon. This is the tallest, largest and most impressive of the 100 pine species. Its cones greatly impressed David Douglas, British botanist-explorer who gathered seeds in 1826 to send to England from Oregon sugar pines 245 feet tall.

Western white pine (<u>Pinus monticola</u>) has the second longest cones in the Northwest, up to 10 inches. Both tree species bear few cones, very high up, and have distinctively scored bark.

7. BROAD-LEAF TREE: The Northwest's largest broad-leaf tree, one of the tallest and largest broad-leafs in North America is the black cottonwood (<u>Populus trichocarpa</u>). Largest west of the Cascades-- 175' high and 4 to 5' in diameter-- it is also the largest broad-leaf tree east of the Cascades. It can tolerate the widest range of moisture of any Northwest tree- 140 inches of rain on the coast, 6 to 8 inches in the interior, where it grows only along lakes and streams.

THE MOST EXTENSIVE

1. FORESTS: Western Washington and northwestern Oregon have the most extensive, densest forests in the U.S., and the nation's most commercially productive conifer forests. No other area has such large and long-lived individual trees of so many diverse conifer species. Oregon has the nation's most valuable reserve of standing timber. Of its 13 national forests totaling 15.6 million acres, Willamette N.F., which includes four Wilderness areas, has the nation's largest national forest timber acreage and harvest.

2. PINE AND JUNIPER: Idaho has the world's most extensive stands of western white pine. Oregon has one of the world's most extensive stands of western juniper near Redmond (106,138 acres); the world's only major stands of Port-Orford-cedar; the Northwest's only myrtle groves and the world's most northerly stand of redwoods, all in the extreme southwest corner. Washington has more than half the nation's western redcedar, and 40% of its western hemlock. Western Oregon and northern Idaho both have prime stands of western redcedar.

3. EELGRASS: Two of the most extensive beds of eelgrass (Zostera nolti) on the West Coast, if not in the world, grow in Washington waters, one at Willapa Bay, the other at Padilla Bay near Bellingham. Thick colonies of the grass, always partially submerged, also are found in many sheltered Puget Sound inlets.
    Eelgrass, a pioneering land plant that edged out into the sea, is one of only a few flowering plants in the world that grow in saltwater. The flowers open under water, their pollen is waterborne, and the seeds are dispersed by the tides.

It also spreads by creeping rhizomes and roots that mat and stabilize the soil while enriching it with decaying organic material. Eelgrass shelters many lower intertidal and subtidal organisms; food washed in constantly by the tides benefits clams, shrimps, small snails and worms. Residents include hydroids, tiny sea urchins and sea anemones, numerous sedentary jellyfish, and small scallops anchored with a secreted thread, filter-feeding on tiny organic particles.

Among nudibranch species living in and on the eelgrass is one, found nowhere else, only 1½" long, black-and-white striped, and narrow, matching the width and striping of the blades.

Eelgrass beds are vital to larger animals such as salmon, crab and flatfish, which attract harbor seals. They are also vital to hundreds of thousands of migrating and wintering waterfowl and shorebirds, such as ducks, Canada geese and black brant. All feed on the grass, seeds and small animals living there.

THE MOST FIRE-RESISTANT

TREE: The most fire- and drought-resistant Pacific Northwest tree is the ponderosa pine (Pinus ponderosa) which grows almost exclusively east of the Cascades in areas with only 8 to 12 inches of rain. Even small trees have tap roots 3 to 5 feet long. The hardy trees, which live to be 400 to 500 years old, can tolerate a scorchingly hot ground surface (162° F.). Older trees have such thick bark that they can survive many fires. A healthy 250-year-old ponderosa pine cut in Idaho showed the scars of 21 fires. Douglas fir, with bark as thick as 12 inches thick, also resists fire well.

THE MOST NUMEROUS

1. **NATIONAL FORESTS:** Oregon has the most national forests in the Northwest-- 13, with 16,073,563 acres. Boise N.F. is the Northwest's largest with 2.6 million acres. A close second is Idaho's Challis N.F. with 2,535,590 acres. Third is Washington's Wenatchee N.F. with 2,464,068 acres. Idaho has the most acreage: 20,741,808 in 10 national forests. These include Idaho Panhandle N.F., made up of three former national forests.

2. **MOSSES/LICHENS:** Olympic Peninsula rain forests have the most species (70) and individuals of epiphytes of any area equal in size in the lower 48. The number of species would be greater except for occasional summer droughts a month or two long. Epiphytes-- air plants-- manufacture their own food, extracting water for the process from the air, usually well saturated in rain forests.
   Their host is used only for a support. Bigleaf maple is the most heavily draped tree; its large branches and rough bark allow secure attachment. Wet epiphytes on one large tree can weigh a ton or more. Many grow only at certain levels, preferring crown, branches or a spot near the base. Others drape trees and logs everywhere.

3. **MUSHROOMS:** With ideal conditions for mushrooms in the damp, forested Northwest, Washington and Oregon produce the most chanterelles of any state in the nation. Many hundreds of mushroom species have already been identified in Washington. Idaho and inland areas have such mushrooms as Boletus edulus, one of a dozen very edible Northwest fungi. Often weighing 4 or 5 pounds, it grows to record size in inland coniferous forests, up to 10 pounds and 12" across the cap.

THE EARLIEST

1. WILDFLOWERS: Among the Northwest's earliest, most accessible and beautiful high-elevation wild-flowers is the glacier lily (<u>Erythronium grandi-florum</u>). It pushes up through snow, aided by a tissue temperature 27° F. warmer than its surroundings. The nodding, clear yellow petals grace damp mountain meadows both west and east of the Cascades, down to northern Oregon.

2. Also growing up through snow, often next to the glacier lily, avalanche lilies (<u>Erythronium montanum</u>) flower by the hundreds in damp, high-mountain meadows. Pure white except for yellow at the throat, they can be seen in the Olympics at Hurricane Ridge and Obstruction Point during July. They also grow in meadows of the Cascades of Washington and Oregon, south to Mt. Hood. With so short a summer, each plant stores up enough energy to bloom and form seed only every six years.

THE WIDEST ELEVATION RANGE

TREE: Engelmann spruce (Picea engelmannii) grows in the widest elevation range of any Pacific Northwest tree, from 1700 feet (in northern Idaho) to 9000 feet. Still tall at timberline, it seldom grows very far west of the Cascade Divide.

THE FASTEST GROWING

TREE: Red alder (Alnus rubra) is the Northwest's fastest-growing tree in its early stages. In 5 years it can reach 15 feet, in 10 years, 35 to 40 feet. Maximum height before rot sets in is 100 to 110 feet. It is one of the most prolific growers of Northwest coastal trees.

Among conifers, Douglas fir is the fastest grower west of the Cascades; during a competition in 1975, a leader on the winning Douglas fir grew 61.8 inches in one season. Western white pine and western larch grow fastest east of the Cascades, where few red alders grow.

Red alder seldom exceeds 20 inches in diameter yet it is the largest of the alders, the most valuable hardwood tree west of the Cascades, and the only commercially harvested tree in the Northwest that is more abundant now than a century ago.

Clean-burning and not pitchy, red alder is the most popular wood for fireplaces and barbecues.

A substance in the bark used by Northwest Indians to cure rheumatic fever is used by doctors today for the same purpose.

The alder is unique among Northwest trees in having root nodules that improve forest soils; conifers grow more rapidly where red alder has grown. It absorbs nitrogen from the air and converts it into soil nitrogen used by other plants as alder leaf litter decomposes.

THE RICHEST AND RAREST

The Pacific Northwest has some of the richest concentrations of the rarest plant species in the West-- sometimes in the world. Many are alpine flora, isolated by Ice Age glaciers, that now survive only on mountain tops or canyon cliffs. Some more southerly plants migrated north during warm periods between cold spells, then were isolated.

1. Most widely scattered may be the Olympic onion (Allium crenulatum), found only on high peaks in the Olympic Mountains, east to the Wenatchee Mountains, and in southwest Oregon on the two highest peaks of the Coast Range-- Saddle Mountain (3287') and Mary's Peak (4,097'), often among other rare alpine flora. The onion has brilliant rose-purple flowers and narrow leaves that may curl in at the tip.

2. The Wenatchee Mountains are rich in species limited to a certain area. Tumwater Canyon Botanical Area has been set aside to protect Lewisia tweedyi, rarest and largest of the Lewisias, which grows naturally only in those mountains up to 5000 feet high. The lovely saucer-shaped blooms with up to 12 petals 1½" to 3" in diameter vary in color from pale pink to apricot. The fleshy tap root extends 3' into talus slopes and rock crevices where soil is only a few inches deep. The hardy plant withstands temperatures between -30° to 100° F.

3. COLUMBIA RIVER GORGE: Of 800 plant species in the Gorge, 58 are rare or endangered; nine may

exist nowhere else because of the wide range of
climate, dry at the east end, wet at the west end.
It is one of few places where alpine plants
flourish at sea level, survivors of the last ice
age. During the cold periods, plants survived
high on Gorge cliffs, often near waterfalls. On
both sides of the river toward the east end of the
Gorge, the rare Penstemon barrettae gray displays 1½-inch-long, purplish blooms on basaltic
cliff faces, talus slopes and flat rocky soil. It
survives the dryness with fan-shaped roots that
spread out 4' and thrust 2' deep to search for
water and food. Its leathery leaves, 1 to 5" long,
are the showiest of all penstemon leaves, silver-
green in summer, purple-bronze in winter.

On the Washington side is one of the densest
concentrations of rare plant species in the Gorge,
with nine rare plants endemic to the area. On dry
hillsides grow a few plants of the obscure butter-
cup (Ranunculus reconditus).

About 1000 plants of the Columbia River milk-
vetch (Astragalus columbianus), believed extinct in 1975 after Priest Rapids Dam was built,
were found in 1980, growing between Hanford Reservation and the U.S. Military Yakima Firing Range.

Several rare grassland communities including
threatened or endangered combinations of Idaho
fescue, threetipped sagebrush and antelope bitter-
brush are protected in Washington and Oregon.

Oregon has many rare plant "islands." On
22½-acre Camassia Natural Area atop West Linn's
high basalt bluff, grow 300 species of plants rare
in northern Oregon. Lower Table Top, a mile-long,
eroded basaltic mesa in Table Rock Wilderness Area
has 9 rare or endangered species, including dwarf
meadow foam, growing only beside pools that form
on the summit in spring. Little Blitzen Research
Natural Area, one of several deep, glacier-carved
valleys on Steens Mountain, highest fault block
in the Northwest, has a rich concentration of
plants rare in the region.

Oregon's largest population of the very rare giant western bog lily (Lilium occidentale), which grows only in sphagnum bogs and wetlands on southern Oregon and adjacent California coasts, is protected in Bastendorf Bog.

Carlisle Bog in Washington's Grays Harbor County has two rare plants: swamp sandwort (Arenaria paludicola) and Menzie's burnet (Sanguisorba menzieii), as well as the Olympic mudminnow.

Southwestern Oregon's Klamath-Siskiyou area is a botanist's dream area, containing a fourth of Oregon's rare or endangered plants. Two climatic zones meet there-- coastal fog and arid interior mountain slopes and valleys. Eight Dollar Mountain, with both bog and grassland, also has many rare plants, including Epilobium oreganum.

In the same area rugged Kalmiopsis Wilderness is home to Kalmiopsis leachiana, one of the world's rarest shrubs. Twelve species of conifers growing there include rare Port-Orford-cedar and Brewer weeping spruce (Picea breweriana). This pre-Ice Age relic of a swampy, subtropical era is found in the Brewer Spruce Research Natural Area 4000 to 8000 feet high. The 50-to-75' tall spruce with droopy limbs grows only on serpentine soil. In the Siskiyous is the nation's largest outcrop of serpentine rock, thrust up long ago from deep ocean floor. A dozen wildflowers grow only on that soil.

Away from the coastal fog belt, in Josephine and Curry Counties, grows the rare Iris innominata, discovered only in 1928. Its blooms are veined in a deeper tone of the main color: bronze, yellow, or purple.

An exceptional diversity of plants (300 species) and habitats is found in Washington's Bald Hill Preserve at the edge of the Puget lowland, with important plants typical of glacial outwash prairies of South Puget Sound. Rarest plants are

the threatened giant Trillium albidum and Nut-
tall's quillwort, once believed eradicated from
Washington. In close proximity are old-growth
coniferous forests (with Douglas fir up to 8' in
diameter and more than 250 years old); white oak
woodland and savannah; rock outcrops, cliffs and
boulders; open grass-covered "balds;" riparian deciduous forests, wetlands and a lake. Western
redcedar, bigleaf maple, Pacific dogwood, grand
fir, Pacific madrone, western hemlock all thrive
in the richly varied habitats.

Unique plant species evolved on peaks of the
Olympic mountains which have been isolated and
scoured by mountain glaciers. A dozen alpine
species, found only in the Olympics-- some only on
Hurricane Ridge-- survived both the ice ages and
the warmer climate afterwards, clinging to high
ridges above 5500 feet.

Best known is Piper's harebell
(Campanula piperi), rated as one of
the rarest and most beautiful of
all western campanulas. Even
when blooming, with clear blue
flowers ½ to 1" wide, it is only
2" high. Scattered on high rocky talus
slopes, it roots in fine crevices,
protected against strong winds. Because
it needs abundant moisture, the harebell
often grows near the snout of a glacier.

Among other endemic Olympic wildflowers are
Flett's violet (Viola flettii), a true violet
also found in Washington's Cascades and Wenatchee
Mountains, and the only endangered Olympic plant,
Astragalus cottoni. Daisy-like Senecio flet-
tii grows only on Mount Angeles, often on talus.

In the Yakima River Basin grow 20 plant species found only in Washington, 10 of them found
nowhere else but in the Basin. Growing only on
basaltic cliffs in Yakima River Canyon, rooted in
crevices, is Erigeron basalticus, a low-altitude
perennial with pink-purple daisylike flowers.

THE MOST UNEXPECTED

1. PLANT LIFE: Scientists believed that the ashfall and blast of scorching air accompanying the eruption of Mount St. Helens in 1980 had so sterilized the soil that no plants would grow there for many years. By 1983, 230 of nearly 300 species formerly in the area had reappeared.

Within four months, plant life appeared in many areas, except where pyroclastic flows covered the soil. Some plants were seeded naturally by wind or mud. A number of small trees and other plants survived, including a few clumps of lupine in a blast area. Some were protected by heavy layers of snow on north-facing slopes. Evidently ash stimulated rather than stunted plant growth.

The first fall rains in 1980 brought small black mushrooms (<u>Anthracobia melatoma</u>), which must have found organic material in the ash. By breaking down such material, fungi help build soil for higher plants. Farther down the mountain, shell fungi soon appeared on blown-down trees; the mycellia were insulated deep inside the wood. Even conifers returned. Two years after the blast, noble fir seedlings were seen. All plant life thrived during the wet cool summer of 1983.

Soil fertility was enhanced by the bodies of large animals that died in the blast, and by many mounds of deep, rich earth pushed up by pocket gophers, which survived the blast underground.

Fireweed, one of the first plants to sprout in burned-over areas, soon appeared. And so did soil-building Columbian lupine, rooting in six inches of ash. Bear grass and the sapprophyte Indian pipe also returned.

Some grasses and trees were planted to stabilize the mudflow. But there will be no planting within the 110,300 acres national volcanic monument area. There, nature will be allowed to heal itself in a rare outdoor laboratory.

2. PLANTS IN LAVA: One of the most unexpected sights for visitors to Idaho's bleak Craters of the Moon National Monument is plant life. Growing on the lava are more than 200 plant species such as rabbit brush, bitterroot, sagebrush, pink monkeyflower, dwarf buckwheat, and syringa. Although trees are slow-growing, there are firs, quaking aspen, junipers and many limberpines.

Protected by a dry climate, the lava looks much more recent than it is. The rings of the 1500-year-old Triple-twist tree, a silvery snag that grew in a crevice, accurately date the area.

TRIPLE TWIST TREE DATES LAVA
IN 1954 SCIENTISTS COUNTED 1350 GROWTH RINGS ON
A 18.5" CORE FROM THIS GNARLED LIMBER PINE   THE
ESTIMATED AGE IS 1,500 YEARS BECAUSE THE HEART WAS
ROTTED AWAY ALLOWING ANOTHER 100 YEARS FOR AMPLE
SOIL TO COLLECT FOR GROWTH OF THE SEED THIS LAVA
MAY HAVE FLOWED IN THE FOURTH CENTURY

PART THREE

THE PHYSICAL WORLD

THE HIGHEST

1. MOUNTAIN PASS: The five highest mountain passes in the Pacific Northwest are all in Idaho: Galena Summit, 8701'; Teton Pass, 8429'; Targhee Pass, 7072'; Gibbons Pass, 6995'; Monida Pass, 6823'. The view of the Sawtooth Range from Galena Summit is rated one of the most spectacular mountain views in the Pacific Northwest.

2. MONOLITH: Beacon Rock is the Northwest's highest monolith-- a single rock formation detached from bedrock, protruding from the earth's surface. Covering 17 acres, rising 848 feet from the Washington shore of the Columbia River, it is said to be the world's second largest monolith. Older than the Cascades, it is probably a volcano plug that eroded away except for the clogged conduit. A steep, one-mile trail to the top, with 52 hairpin turns and 22 wooden bridges, offers a superb view of the gorge.

3. FAULTS: Highest and largest exposed fault in North America is Abert Rim, one of southeastern Oregon's best-known geological features. Formed of many layers of lava cracked by deep internal pressure and thrust up into a huge tilted block, the 30-mile-long, barely eroded escarpment rises 2000' from the desert floor on its west side.

4. RIVER: The world's highest navigable river is Idaho's St. Joe River, which passes through three lakes before emptying into Lake Coeur d'Alene. It cuts across the Panhandle at 2100', meandering for its final 72 miles. Once, stern wheelers traveled on the slower parts. Now, long log rafts move on it to sawmills on Lake Coeur d'Alene's shores.

5. MOUNTAIN: Mount Rainier, the highest mountain
in the Northwest at 14,410', is the highest volcano and the fifth highest peak in the lower 48. The
most impressive Cascade volcano, with the greatest
mass, it dominates the landscape. No other U.S.
mountain rises so far above its foothills.

The broad mountain mass has three high points:
Columbia Crest, 14,410', located where two relatively recent craters overlap; Point Success,
14,150'; Liberty Cap, 14,112'.

Once nearly 16,000' high, Mount Rainier was
lowered by several huge mudflows, including the
world's largest, Osceola. During this century,
rock avalanches and extensive mudflows have poured
down its slopes.

Mount Rainier provides some of the lower 48's
most popular and also, most difficult climbs.

*MOUNT RAINIER: lower 48's highest volcano, greatest mass of any
Cascade volcano (Washington State Tourism)*

6. WATERFALL: Oregon's Multnomah Falls is the highest in the Northwest, 4th highest in the U.S. Its two tiers cascade 620' over steep cliffs of basalt in the Columbia Gorge. Its source is a stream 4 miles long, born 3200' up in the mountains. The waterfall was discovered in 1792 by Lt. Broughton of Captain Vancouver's expedition.

7. FAULT BLOCK: Steens Mountain is the highest fault block in the U.S., 30 miles long, so high at 9670' that it has five life zones. Rising almost without foothills above grassland and sage-brush, Steens is a classic fault block, with the western side rising gently, 5000 feet in 20 miles, and the nearly perpendicular eastern side rising to that height in only three miles. A loop drive to the summit ascends the western side. A number of hot springs issue from its base.

The region's highest mountain, formed of 100 lava flows, one of few mountains in southeastern Oregon that had glaciers, Steens has glacier-carved valleys and snow-filled cirques in which a dozen small streams, and the Donner and Blitzen Rivers, originate. They run down the gentle slope into Malheur Lake, the nation's largest fresh-water marsh. The lake is an essential part of Malheur National Wildlife Refuge, created in 1908, one of the nation's largest at 183,000 acres. Many thousands of migrating waterfowl of 250 species rest and feed there twice a year.

THE DEEPEST

1. LIMESTONE CAVE: The Northwest's deepest limestone cave, the world's 4th deepest, is Idaho's Papoose Cave, located near Hells Canyon. Nearly 1000 feet deep, very cold and wet, it has beautiful limestone formations.

2. LAKE: Our nation's deepest lake, 2nd deepest
on the continent, 7th deepest in the world, is
Oregon's Crater Lake, 1932' deep. Located within
a volcanic caldera 5 miles across and 4000' deep,
it is one of the most beautiful of all lakes,
discovered in 1853, and now the heart of Crater
Lake National Park, at 6176' altitude.

It has no inlet or outlet. Water level, varying less than 3' a year, is maintained by evapora-
tion and seepage, and a 50' annual snowfall.

Crater Lake fills the caldera of ancient Mount
Mazama, once a Cascade volcano. A series of violent pumice and ash eruptions 6845 years ago emptied the volcano's magma chamber, causing the summit to collapse. More volcanic activity occurred
inside the resulting caldera. Wizard Island, a
cinder cone from the last eruption, rising from
the caldera floor to 764' above the water, may be
3000 years old. Rocks on 161'-high Phantom Ship,
part of a peak built earlier than the main mass of
Mount Mazama, are the oldest visible Mazama flow.

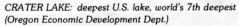

CRATER LAKE: deepest U.S. lake, world's 7th deepest
(Oregon Economic Development Dept.)

3. CANYON: Deepest and most rugged river gorge in North America is Hells Canyon, a natural border between northeastern Oregon and Idaho. For more than 40 miles the average canyon depth is 5500' from rim to water. In Idaho canyon walls rise 8032'; in Oregon, more than a mile at Hat Point.

The Snake River, 1000 miles long and a major tributary of the Columbia River, cut the huge canyon after the last flood basalts, 13 million years ago. Proof lies in upper canyon walls that show 4000' of the old flows, with prominent ledges and vertical columns. The lower walls reveal older, light-colored sedimentary rocks, once a continental shelf of the Pacific Ocean floor.

Like the Columbia River, the Snake cut its way through a rising mountain range, the Blue Mountains, eroding very hard greenstone. Aiding it at

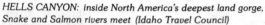

HELLS CANYON: inside North America's deepest land gorge, Snake and Salmon rivers meet (Idaho Travel Council)

one time was floodwater from ancient Lake Bonneville, pouring down a valley near Pocatello.

Below its three dams, Hells Canyon contains
the last primitive part of the Snake River, with
70 miles of rapids alternating with deep pools. At
peak flow, river waves within the canyon can be
12' high. Most of the 67 miles of the Snake that
are part of the National Wild and Scenic River
System lie within Hells Canyon Recreation Area.

Canyon walls can be gently rolling hills or
step-like terraces; shores can be gravel bars or
sandy shelves. Often lava differs on each side of
the canyon, because cones formed by volcanic eruptions in the Snake River Plains made the river me-
ander, often forcing it to cut its channel between
overlapping cones.

As the river erodes and carries rock down-
stream, the load on the earth's crust lightens,
and plateau and mountains above the canyon rise.

The canyon is so deep that the climate within
it is milder than the climate on the rim. Indians
wintered down in the canyon, digging pit dwellings
on larger terraces or living in caves gouged in
canyon walls by swift water. Artifacts and drawings on cave walls document human use.

THE LONGEST

1. **SANDSPIT:** The longest natural sandspit in the
U.S. is Washington's Dungeness Spit, curving into
the Strait of Juan de Fuca 5½ miles, between Port
Angeles and Sequim on the Olympic Peninsula. Down
the center of the spit, 100 yards wide, is a wall
of driftwood 10' high. One of the Northwest's
oldest lighthouses is at its tip, which narrows
and curls to the northeast. Graveyard Spit hooks
away from the main spit toward the mainland.

Lying within the Olympic rain shadow, the spit
is one of the driest places on the coast north of

San Diego, with only 15" of rain a year.

Wave action keeps the spit narrow at the land end; winter storms may even temporarily breach it. The spit was formed, and is rebuilt, from material eroded by waves from soft sea cliffs along the Strait, and from sediment carried by the Elwha and Dungeness Rivers. It grows 10 to 20 feet a year.

On the western outer shore, exposed to the Strait and prevailing winds, the surf is rough. Along the inner shore, the water is calm and shallow, protected by two spits.

Dungeness National Wildlife Area attracts 275 bird species, making the spit one of the nation's top bird-watching spots. 40,000 migrating birds rest and feed there. Offshore eelgrass beds to the north shelter many small animals. Young salmon from the rivers feed in the harbor for a year or two before going out to sea. In no other area on the Strait did so many Indians settle, lured by the food supply.

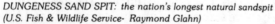

DUNGENESS SAND SPIT: the nation's longest natural sandspit
(U.S. Fish & Wildlife Service- Raymond Glahn)

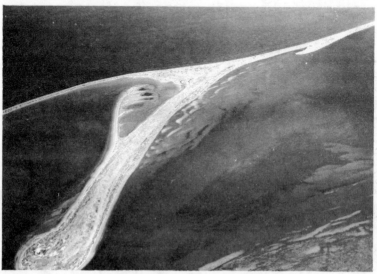

3. ROADLESS SEACOAST: Washington has the lower 48's longest roadless seacoast, most undeveloped and primitive Pacific Ocean shore, and its last undisturbed coastal ecosystem. From Cape Flattery south to Kalaloch, the narrow 57-mile-long roadless shore is either Indian land or Olympic National Park, the Northwest's most visited national park, the only one in the U.S. that offers high mountains, seashore and conifer forests.

Washington's many inlets, islands, bays and inland sea give it one of the nation's longest saltwater shorelines, 3026 undulating miles.

The northern seacoast is rocky, rugged and inaccessible with wave-eroded benches and seacliffs, offshore sea stacks, stone arches, islands and islets. Some are remnants of ancient oceanic plate.

POINT OF ARCHES: most beautiful spot of nation's longest, most undeveloped sea coast, off the Olympic Peninsula (Bob & Ira Spring)

4. LAVA CAVE: The longest unbroken lava cave in
the Western Hemisphere is Ape Cave, 12,810' long.
It lies on the southern flank of Mount St. Helens
within a 7-mile-long lava flow, 1900 years old.
Three other lava caves in the same area are the
next longest in the lower 48. Lava caves are
numerous in all three Northwest states. Some have
permanent ice inside them, especially in Idaho.

Lava caves form when a flow cools enough to
crust over while the lava underneath remains hot
enough to continue flowing. Gradually the level
of the interior lava river drops, leaving a tube
filled with hot gases, and then, an empty passage.
The falling levels leave ridges on the walls.

Ape Cave, discovered in 1951, was not mapped
until 1978. It has no multiple levels and few
side passages, but interesting features, such as
lava falls, lava-cicles, iridescent fungus, and
ripples. Unique to it are a lava ball left above
floor-level by lava flowing at a higher level, and
several other lava balls stuck together.

5. RIVER: The Columbia River is the longest in
the lower 48-- 1243 miles. It is the largest riv-
er in North America flowing into the Pacific.
Among the rivers of the lower 48, it is second in
volume only to the Mississippi-Missouri system.
Draining 258,000 miles, most of those miles in the
Northwest, it empties the most water into the
Pacific of any river in the Western Hemisphere.

The huge amount of water dilutes the Pacific
Ocean as far as 300 miles offshore, giving sensory
clues to salmon and steelhead heading back to
spawn. Unlike most rivers, its greatest flow is
in spring and early summer, because of snowmelt.

The Columbia, perhaps 100 million years old,
predates the Cascade Range. The powerful river,
scouring its channel through hard basalt, kept
pace as the mountains rose 4500' above the river.
Only the Columbia breached that range.

Only such major obstacles as giant lava flows and continental ice sheets have diverted the mighty river. Huge landslides on Washington's side of the Gorge, and lava from modern volcanoes have blocked the river, but only briefly.

The West's longest commercial waterway, the Columbia was a convenient waterway and gathering place for thousands of years for widely scattered Indian tribes who came to fish and to trade.

It was discovered in 1792 by Captain Robert Gray, who suspected that the "River of the West" might be the cause of discolored water he saw far out at sea. He found the river mouth, sailed over the bar under full sail, and claimed the river for the U.S., strengthening our hand during the 1846 boundary negotiations with Britain. Gray sailed some 15 miles upstream, traded with Indians for sea otter furs, filled his water casks, and caulked his ship, the Columbia Rediviva.

Lewis and Clark, the first Americans to reach the mouth of the river, mapped it as they traveled on it, and wrote in their journals about the large number of Indian dugout canoes on it. By the 1850s, steamboats used the Columbia, as the only level road between interior and ocean.

Now the Columbia is the largest source of hydroelectric power in North America, with 11 major dams and more than 100 others on its tributaries. Before it was dammed, it dumped the most sediment in the ocean of any Western Hemisphere river-- 7.5 million tons a year. The sediment is gouged from Cascade volcanoes by glaciers and brought to the Columbia by tributaries. Over the centuries, that sediment created Pacific beaches, Long Beach Peninsula, and one of the world's most treacherous river mouth sandbars, especially during winter storms. It has caused more than 2000 shipwrecks and 1500 deaths. Storms, winds up to 160 mph, and erratic currents made that area one of the most feared stretches of navigable water in the world for sailing ships-- the Graveyard of the Pacific.

COLUMBIA RIVER GORGE: one of world's most outstanding
river gorges (Oregon Economic Development Dept.)

THE MOST OUTSTANDING

1. GORGE: The 85-mile-long Columbia River Gorge
is one of the Northwest's natural wonders, one of
the world's most outstanding river gorges, scenic-
ally and geologically. Cut by a mighty river, it
is the only sea-level breach in the 600-mile-long
Cascade Range. Steep river-gouged walls reveal
Northwest geology, the many layers of flood basalt
that built the Columbia Plateau, the tilting of
some layers as the Cascades were built. The river
was much older than the volcanoes, and maintained
its channel as the mountains rose. The walls tell
of a vastly swollen river during the world's largest floods, scouring cliffs, widening the gorge as
it roared out toward the sea.
　　Over steep cliffs on the Oregon side pour the
world's largest concentration of waterfalls,

including Multnomah Falls, highest in the Northwest. Forty miles of one of the most scenic roads
in the U.S. passes nine major falls in ten miles.
    Within the gorge two different climates col-
lide, dry and often bitterly cold from the east,
moist and warmer from the west. Winds blowing at
a steady 15 to 25 mph may cause winter ice storms
in Portland. Vegetation within the gorge reflects
the contrasting amount of moisture, and includes
many rare plant survivors of the Ice Age.

2. ISLAND CHAIN: Perhaps the most outstandingly
beautiful chain of islands in the world is the San
Juan Archipelago, spreading out for 30 miles in
Washington's inland sea. At low tide 768 rocks,
islands, and reefs are exposed; at high tide, 475.
There are 175 named islands. San Juan County is
one of only two U.S. counties composed entirely of
islands.   State ferries from the nation's largest
ferry system run regularly to Lopez, San Juan and
Orcas. Some of the eight larger islands have
coves, lakes, meadows, swamps, harbors, beaches.
    The islands are the tops of drowned mountains
in a range once connecting Vancouver Island with
the mainland. The area was scoured several times
by huge lobes of glacial ice flowing south from
western British Columbia mountains. The Fraser
Glaciation, the last, buried the islands in ice
which carved out deep channels with steep sides.
These became underwater cliffs after the ice melted and salt water filled the channels. Many of
the islands show signs of glaciation-- bedrock
grooved or polished, cliffs and shorelines eroded,
huge alien boulders left in glacial deposits.
    Largest island by one square mile is Orcas,
shaped like a warped M. Heavily forested, with
many bays and coves, it has the highest peak of
the islands, Mount Constitution, 2409 feet. The
360° view of islands and snowy peaks from that
summit, covered with ice ½ mile thick during the

final glaciation, is one of the world's most scenic marine views. The archipelago is located within the Olympic rain shadow, the nation's best known. Annual rainfall ranges from 15 to 29".

San Juan Island, county seat and second largest island, has rocks up to 300 million years old, including a small, fossil-rich piece of Asia, carried there by tectonic plates.

That island was the last U.S. territory to be occupied by the British during the peaceful, 13-year-long "Pig War," which began in 1859, 13 years after the 1846 boundary settlement with Britain. The real cause of the "war" was not the killing of a pig but unclear boundaries. Although British warships anchored off the coast, both sides fraternized on major holidays from their separate camps, now preserved as San Juan Island National Historical Park. In 1872 arbitrator Kaiser Wilhelm I set the boundary in mid-Haro Strait.

SAN JUAN ISLANDS: world's most outstandingly beautiful chain of islands (Bob & Ira Spring)

OREGON CAVES: West Coast's largest, most impressive limestone cave; most varied formations for its size (Bob & Ira Spring)

3. CAVE: Oregon's most outstanding cave is Oregon Caves, nationally known for so many varied limestone formations in so small an area. Isolated high in the Siskiyous near Grants Pass, the cave is the West Coast's largest and most impressive limestone cave open to the public.

It is the Northwest's only cave formed in marble-- the only block of marble within several states, 40 miles long. It has many flowstone draperies and canopies, formed as weakly acidic water drips through fractured marble and flows over rock, depositing a thin calcite layer.

The cave has 5 levels, a creek, and 3 miles of passages. Half a mile, much of it narrow and low-roofed, is open for tours. Largest room is the Ghost Room, 40' high, 50' wide, and 250' long. The interconnected chambers are filled with rock waterfalls and chandeliers; soda straw, grape, and popcorn shapes; fluted and pipe-organ columns.

4. LAKE: One of the Northwest's most outstanding lakes is Washington's fjord-like Lake Chelan, 55 miles long, ¼ to 2 miles wide. One of the Northwest's deepest lakes at 1600', it fills a classic glacial valley with gently sloping hillsides. A glacial moraine dams the lower end of the valley, which was buried many thousands of years ago nearly to the top of its highest peaks by an ice sheet extending to the Columbia River.

As the valley glacier receded, the lowland ice sheet, continuing to advance, dammed the valley's mouth. Meltwater and water drained down hillsides and formed the lake, fed today by 59 streams and 27 active glaciers of the North Cascades.

At the northern end of the lake, roadless and ruggedly beautiful country adjoins North Cascades National Park. The lake is unique in the nation as a "waterway to Wilderness;" thousands of acres around Lake Chelan are federal Wilderness, accessible only by boat.

5. SERPENTINE ROCK: The most outstanding slab of serpentine rock exposed in the Northwest, perhaps in the world, is central Oregon's Canyon Mountain near the John Day fossil beds. Normally this weak green rock, called soapstone for its greasy feel, is found in the lower part of the ocean floor beneath a layer of basalt flows. Soft enough to cut with a knife, it is highly polished, the result of slipping and flowing under pressure.

Millions of years ago when the ocean floor was sinking and sliding under the continent, serpentinite slabs could be folded up into continental mountains. This mountainous slab of nearly intact ocean crust stands on edge.

Twin Sisters Mountain near Mount Baker is one of the nation's most remarkable rock bodies, a 10 by 3 mile solid mass of dunite, consisting mostly of the mineral olivine. Not an igneous rock, it could be a recrystallized form of serpentinite.

6. MARINE DRIVE: The nation's, and perhaps the world's, most outstanding scenic marine drive runs 362 miles down Oregon's coast, usually within sight of the sea. Alongside most of the road is one of the Northwest's best bicycle trails.

Although the beach is often accessible by trail, this coast is one of the least developed coastlines in the lower 48. The drive offers a variety of scenery: wind-sculpted sand dunes, jutting lava headlands (capes), river mouths, coves, freshwater lakes, wind-twisted trees, sea lions sunning on rocky ledges, beaches piled with driftwood, tide pools rich in marine animals, lighthouses, and huge offshore boulders.

State charters of Washington and Oregon provide for holding beaches in public trust, and most ocean beaches in both states are public. Oregon's private beaches must allow public access.

OREGON COAST at Bandon: largest grouping of rocks on nation's most outstanding scenic marine drive (Saling)

THE MOST EXTENSIVE

1. WATERFALLS: The most extensive group of large and accessible waterfalls in North America, perhaps in the world, plunges over basalt cliffs along Oregon's Columbia Gorge Scenic Highway. In all, there are 70 waterfalls on the south side of the gorge, most within 20 miles of each other. The Road of Falling Waters passes nine major falls in 10 miles, only 100 miles from Portland.

Two-tiered Multnomah Falls is highest in the Northwest, 4th highest in the U.S., at 620'. Latourelle Falls drops 249', Elowah Falls, 289'.

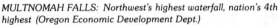

MULTNOMAH FALLS: Northwest's highest waterfall, nation's 4th highest (Oregon Economic Development Dept.)

The Northwest's largest waterfall, and one of the most spectacular at full flow in spring and early summer, when not diverted for power production, is Idaho's Shoshone Falls on the Snake River 4½ miles east of Twin Falls. It drops 212' from a 1000' wide, horseshoe-shaped, basaltic rim.

Most of Idaho's waterfalls have their origin in glaciation-- breaking through and pouring over moraines and plunging down glacial valley walls.

Some 700 falls have been mapped in the Northwest, but hundreds more may yet be discovered in rugged wilderness country. The Northwest has so many waterfalls partly because of ample water from rain and snowmelt, and partly because of the lava cliffs over which so many plunge.

The sheer basalt cliffs hanging hundreds of feet above the water in the Columbia Gorge are the result of the river's cutting through many layers of lava flows alternating with ashfalls. High up on the cliffs, slower-cutting streams eroded only the softer ash, leaving sharp basalt ledges for the water to cascade over.

Oregon has another extensive area of falls accessible by trail in Silver Falls State Park, its largest state park (8502 acres). Of the nine major falls visible along the seven-mile hiking trail that winds through Silver Creek Canyon, five are more than 100' high. In all, the park has 14 falls; highest is South Falls at 177'.

Within or near Mount Rainier National Park are 122 waterfalls, many the result of glaciation. Comet Falls plunges 320' from a hanging valley. Clear Creek and Sluiskin Falls are 300' high.

2. WILDERNESS: Idaho has the most extensive federally classified Wilderness in the Pacific Northwest-- 3,800,000 acres-- and the most undeveloped country and largest Wilderness preserve in the lower 48: 2.2-million-acre River of No Return Wilderness, created in 1980. The Selway-Bitterroot

Wilderness, once the largest, sits atop Idaho's great batholith. It includes three national forests: Bitterroot, Nez Perce, and Clearwater.

MOUNT HEYBURN: part of Idaho's uplifted granite batholith, one of world's most extensive (Idaho Travel Council)

3. BATHOLITH: The Idaho Batholith is the most extensive granite mass in the U.S. and one of the world's largest: 250 miles long and up to 100 miles wide. It dominates the geology of central Idaho where it is uplifted into high, jagged peaks. Batholiths originate as molten rock that cools and crystallizes underground. Later they may be lifted up into mountains or exposed, as on Idaho's lava plains, by erosion.

The Sawtooths are part of that uplifted batholith, their granite peaks sharpened by repeated glacial carving. They are among the most beautiful of all the nation's mountains. Erosion of the Snake River Plains by the Snake, Selway, Salmon, and Lochsa Rivers, each of which cut huge canyons, has exposed 16,000 square miles of the batholith, in a belt 80 miles long.

This intrusion, the largest of Idaho's 11 large granite intrusions, has produced most of the state's mineral wealth. Minerals and ores carried by circulating groundwater tend to concentrate in the cracks and fractures of batholiths, especially near the edges. The Wallowa Batholith in the Blue, Wallowa, and Bald Mountains also produced large amounts of precious metals.

Washington's batholiths still yield some silver and gold. Mount Index Batholith towers above the Skykomish River in Washington near U.S. Highway 2. Mount Stuart Batholith is the oldest in the North Cascades, 80 to 90 million years old. Few large batholiths are as young as Snoqualmie Batholith, only 16 to 18 million years old. Young batholiths at the surface indicate recent vigorous mountain-building, confirming that the Cascades are one of the world's youngest mountain ranges.

4. OBSIDIAN: Oregon's Mount Newberry caldera has within it some of the world's most extensive obsidian flows. The largest and most recent, Big Obsidian Flow, erupted 1350 years ago from the south wall, covering a square mile and leaving a dome over the vent. Its glossy, wrinkled surface ends in cliffs 100 feet high. One flow from a high vent formed a frozen waterfall of obsidian. The several flows are rather recent.

Most obsidian found is young because the rock is unstable and can easily change spontaneously to crystalline form, losing its glassy look. Usually indicating old age in a volcano, the flows are always stiff. A flow from Oregon's Glass Buttes was so viscous it piled up in a mountain at the vent.

Minerals dissolved in Newberry obsidian color it beautifully-- black, brown, red, gold-striped or with a gold or silver sheen.

Dense and rich in silica, obsidian is natural volcanic glass, with few bubbles or crystals. It forms from the same magma as granite, which cools slowly underground. Lack of water is more critical in preventing fully developed crystals than is rapid cooling. One of the driest rocks known, obsidian reaches the surface without much water.

Sometimes black obsidian is topped by a frosting of light-colored pumice, a rock froth related to obsidian but formed from wet magma. At the surface, its steam boils off, leaving the pumice full of small bubbles.

Since the Northwest has little flint for tools and weapons, Northwest Indians traveled long distances for obsidian. It fractures well, with curved surfaces and edges sharper than those of any other cutting tool known. Electronic microscopes show its edge as 500 times sharper than razor blades, and 2 to 3 times as fine and sharp as surgeon's steel and diamond scalpels. Blades of obsidian, fractured by Aztec and Mayan methods, have been used experimentally in delicate surgery on cataracts and brain stems.

5. GEOTHERMAL RESERVOIR: The most extensive subterranean geothermal reservoir of natural steam and hot water underlying any city in the Western Hemisphere allows many residents of Klamath Falls in southwest Oregon to have private geothermal wells in their yard. Indians and early settlers bathed and cooked with water from many hot springs that used to issue freely in the area. The 400 wells drilled in the city's hot spring belt have dried up the springs.

The geothermal water is too corrosive to use directly. City water runs through coils submerged in the hot wells, and then that pure water is used to heat homes, apartments and public buildings; to keep sidewalks, driveways and a critical highway section snow-free; and in industry (for curing

cement and pasteurizing milk, etc.) Near one
private well that is so hot it steams constantly,
a mimosa tree thrives in the greenhouse climate.

*KLAMATH FALLS: underlain by most extensive geothermal reservoir
of any city in Western Hemisphere; a mimosa tree thrives by a
private, steaming, geothermal well (Saling)*

6. AQUIFER: North of the Snake River, the plain
is underlain by one of the world's most extensive
aquifers, the Snake Plains Aquifer, extending for
almost 100 miles northeast from Hagerman Valley.
This aquifer is one of Idaho's most valuable re-
sources, holding hundreds of times more water than
any of its surface reservoirs. The Snake has cut
channels through the aquifer, some of them inter-
secting with it so that springs gush from canyon
walls, forming waterfalls.

One of Idaho's most spectacular sights used to
be Thousand Springs-- hundreds of springs gushing
from a cliff on the north side of Snake River near
Hagerman. Most of the springs are now diverted
for irrigation. Gravity helps feed the aquifer.

The weight of many lava flows and of water in the aquifer caused plains and strata to subside, sloping southwest. The aquifer is made up of many lava layers interbedded with silt, sand and gravel as deep as 3000 feet. Although solid basalt lava lacks the water-holding ability of sedimentary layers, minor folding and faulting has greatly increased the permeability of this lava.

Most aquifer water comes from fairly heavy precipitation in mountains to the southeast. Yet, for more than 250 miles along the south and southeast edges of the plains, no permanent river from the north runs into the Snake River, even though it drains all of Idaho except the extreme southwest. Those rivers, including Big and Little Lost Rivers and Birch Creek, travel underground for more than 100 miles, emerging at last as springs.

THOUSAND SPRINGS: fed by one of world's most extensive aquifers, water gushes from a hillside into Idaho's Snake River (Saling)

7. SAND DUNES: Oregon has the most extensive and spectacular stretch of active coastal sand dunes in the U.S., perhaps in the world. Dunes occupy more than 100 miles of Oregon's 362-mile-long coastline. The best are in Oregon Dunes National Recreation Area, a 40-mile-long stretch between Coos Bay and Florence. Dunes as high as 300 feet extend up to three miles inland.

The Oregon Coast is the only place in the world where so much ocean-related sand is found. Its origin is eroded sediment from coastal mountains, carried to the ocean by three major rivers and smaller streams, and also, sand eroded from exposed sandstone bedrock prevalent in the area.

Ocean currents carry the sediment along the coast, and tides and waves deposit it onto wide, gently sloping beaches. Wind, blowing in a consistent direction at 10 mph or more, picks up the fine sand and adds it to the dunes.

Living sand dunes create a unique environment. As large amounts of sand slip down the steeper surfaces, dunes may whisper, squeak, hum, even boom if they are large enough. They change color with the sun-- gold at dawn, white at noon, pink at sunset. Depending on the season, they flatten or form peaks. Oblique dunes, sometimes with parallel ridges a mile long, are unique to Oregon.

Far from being sterile, Oregon's dunes support 175 species of bird life, and reptiles, mammals and insects. Wildflowers thrive on the edges of inner dunes. The sand, which retains subsurface water, is a cool 60° F. just below the surface.

Living dunes, whose shape constantly changes, gradually move six to 18 feet a year. Winds blow up to 100 mph, carrying sand north in winter, south in summer. Oregon dunes have diverted river mouths, killed stands of trees by overrunning them and blocked the mouths of 17 smaller rivers, forming a chain of freshwater lakes behind the dunes.

Early in the century European beach grass was planted on some dunes near river mouths to try to stabilize them. Unfortunately the grass spread rapidly and soon, shrubs and trees were growing, sending down taproots as deep as 40 feet. Stabilized dunes are dead dunes. Grass can completely cover a dune in 10 to 20 years. Fifty years ago half of Oregon Dunes NRA was open sand; now only a third is. In 100 or 200 years there may be no more living dunes.

All three Northwest states have inland sand dunes in arid country, their material derived from ancient lakebeds and from pumice. Oregon's Christmas Valley has active dunes 60' high next to Lost Forest ponderosa pines. Idaho's golden St. Anthony dunes, 400' high, run north and south a mile wide for 30 miles. Some of Washington's largest and most active inland dunes are protected in Juniper Dunes Wilderness.

OREGON SAND DUNES: Nation's most extensive active coastal sand dunes (Oregon Dept. of Geology & Mineral Industries)

11. GLACIERS: Washington has by far the most extensive network of glaciers in the lower 48-- 135
square miles. Mount Rainier has the most extensive system of glaciers of any single peak in the
lower 48, with 25 named glaciers and 50 smaller
ice patches and secondary glaciers. It has more
snow and ice than any other Cascade volcano. High
as it is, it probably kept its glaciers even during the warmer intervals between ice ages.

When U.S. glaciers were mapped in 1957-58 during the International Geophysical Year, more than
1000 were found. Washington glaciers covered 75%
of the total area. Between Snoqualmie Pass and
the Canadian border 519 glaciers cover more than
97 square miles. 300 are in the North Cascades.

Cascade and Olympic Mountains are uniquely
endowed with huge glaciers, more prevalent on the
coast because of higher peaks, cooler temperatures
and moisture-laden Pacific winds that dump more
than 50 feet of snow a year on the highest peaks.
Pacific winds reaching Idaho are low in moisture.

Glaciers are formed and compacted from snow
that does not melt during the summer. They are
not mere icefields but year-round rivers of ice,
heavy enough to move downhill. When advancing,
they scour the land of topsoil and vegetation;
they groove and polish bedrock, sculpt jagged
peaks, carve out U-shaped valleys.

When retreating, glaciers build land, forming
moraines and hillside terraces, dumping rocky
debris carried in their ice. Their outwash often
fills the lower part of valleys.

During the last glacial period, the valley
glaciers of Mount Rainier were 15 to 40 miles
long. Now, Emmons, the longest and largest, is 5
miles long. Carbon River Glacier, 4.7 miles long,
has scoured out the largest cirque found on any
Cascade peak, with walls rising to summit ice
3600' above. It also has the lowest terminus of
any glacier in the lower 48, 3000', and Rainier's
thickest ice, 705' at 6200' altitude.

Some of Rainier's major glaciers, such as Nisqually, are among the world's most accessible by car or foot. Nisqually is also one of the best-documented glaciers, studied longer than any other in the Western Hemisphere. It was the first U.S. glacier to be reported, discovered during an 1857 ascent of Mt. Rainier. Pictures of it date back to 1884, records of size, to 1857. Between that date and 1944, it retreated 4131'. Now four miles long, it melts readily because of its southern exposure and low terminus, 4000'.

None of Mount Rainier's glaciers is strongly advancing now. Some have advanced slightly since 1950, but the rest remain constant or are retreating. The heavy snows of the early 1970s may account for the slight advances.

MOUNT RAINIER: the lower 48's most extensive system of glaciers on any single peak. Emmons descends from summit at right center, Frying Pan below it, Winthrop at far right, Cowlitz at far left, Ingram to its right (U.S. Geological Survey - Austin Post)

12. BASALT LAVA: The world's most extensive and spectacular accumulation of flood basalt lava forms the Columbia River Plateau. Basaltic lava, which was highly fluid, covered a total of 200,000 square miles in the Pacific Northwest, much of eastern Oregon and eastern Washington, where it ponded against the Cascades. In Idaho, the Snake River Plains, an eastern extension of the Plateau, is the world's second largest accumulation of flood lava, 100 miles wide and 400 miles long, from Weiser to the Wyoming border.

A single flow, the Roza Flow, can be traced for 20,000 square miles, from Grand Coulee east to Spokane, south to Pendleton, and southwest into the Columbia River Gorge. Other flows raced into the northern end of the Willamette valley, on to Portland and then west to the Pacific, extending 40 miles underwater.

Never before or since have there been lava flows of such volume, covering such an extensive area, and with such long intervals between flows-- tens and hundreds of thousands of years. The flows occurred for several million years but hundreds of thousands of years apart, with time between flows for soil and lakes to form, forests to grow. The lakes left their record in white sedimentary layers interbedded between basalt. Red soil layers indicating warm and moist tropical climates are found extensively. Beds of old gravel mark dry climates.

The fluid lava filled canyons, carbonized or encased trees, turned lakes and rivers into steam, dammed streams and created new lakes and swamps. It even diverted the mighty Columbia River. Big Bend, where the river makes a half-circle around the Columbia Basin, was formed when flows pushed the river back repeatedly toward the mountains.

In eastern Washington and northern Oregon most of the flows erupted from an ancient volcano, the Grande Ronde, largest ever known. Swarms of dikes in the Grande Ronde area, which straddles the two

states, indicate the volcano's location. The
dikes-- lava-plugged fractures in the earth that
once served as lava conduits-- were exposed after
softer material around them eroded away.

Basaltic flows in Oregon often have the same
chemical composition and age as flows in southeastern Washington. Scientists can match flows
with sources by comparing the chemical composition
of lava solidified in the dikes with the composition of lava in various flows.

The Columbia Plateau is one of the world's
deepest lava beds. In 1982 a well drilled 16,199
feet near Yakima failed to get below lava into
sedimentary rocks. Even before the Columbia Plateau flows, ancient lava covered much of eastern
Washington. The total depth of the basalt flows
isn't known, but layers 2000 feet deep are visible
in the Snake and Grande Ronde Canyons.

The flows were one of the most important shap-
ing influences on the Northwest landscape east of
the Cascades. Ranging in thickness from a few
feet to several hundred, they leveled the area by
filling in canyons. Often they covered ancient
peaks, the tips of which might later be uncovered
by erosion, so that quartzite or gneiss "islands"
rise from the desert floor, especially on the west
side of the plateau.

Over the leveled land, the very thin lava
spread farther and faster, some flows moving at 25
mph. The weight of the lava caused extreme sub-
sidence in the plateau as well as in the Snake
River Plains, both of which are basins, not pla-
teaus. In Idaho lava flowed from low shield vol-
canos on mile-long fissures located along rifts.

Between flows, layers of lava sometimes folded
or buckled, forming high mountains in Oregon, and
high ridges in Washington, such as Rattlesnake
Hills and Yakima Ridge. Erosion went on between
flows, especially when the climate was warm and
moist. Although basaltic lava is very hard, it
fractures and erodes rather easily.

COLUMNAR JOINTING: Northwest's most unusual lava formation in world's largest flood basalt (Bob & Ira Spring)

THE MOST UNUSUAL

1. LAVA FORMATIONS: The Northwest's most unusual lava formations are 3- to 8-sided pillars, 6" to 2' across, vertical or horizontal, sometimes jack-strawed. They were formed extensively in Columbia Plateau flows. Prime examples of such columnar jointing, 15' in diameter and 200' long, are seen in the walls of upper Grand Coulee. Spokane has some in its central area on river terraces.

Long, straight-sided blocks formed as basaltic lava cooled, both from the top and the bottom. Shrinkage cracks developed and spread inward.

Another curious lava is pillow basalt. When lava flows into fresh water or erupts in the sea, it tends to congeal into cylinders and barrel-like shapes. Later, these may be uplifted and exposed.

2. FOSSIL: Washington's Blue Lake Rhino is one
of the most unusual fossils ever found. The animal mold discovered high in a canyon wall a few
miles south of Dry Falls is the only mammal fossil
ever found in a lava flow. The rhino mold was
discovered in 1935 as an animal-shaped "cave", 3 x
3 x 5 feet, high in a cliff. A jawbone with teeth
and some fragmentary bones found inside the mold
allowed identification. Millions of years ago the
exact shape of a dead rhinoceros was preserved
when one of many Columbia Plateau flows of fluid
basalt invaded a shallow pond in which the animal
was floating, perhaps killed by heat and fumes.
The mold, formed by lava cooling quickly around
the body, shows legs stiffened in death.
      The heat and pressure of the lava flow, about
100' high, would have crushed and burned the body
except for many protective 2'-high basalt pillows,
formed as the lava rapidly cooled upon contact
with the water. Later, the body decomposed within
the lava, and other flows buried the mold. Flood
erosion eventually cut away the lava across the
rump and left hind leg, creating an opening.
      Several types of animals no longer found in
North America lived in the Northwest between one
and 25 million years ago: elephants, small six-
toed horses, giant ground sloths, rhinos, camels.
Remains of many such animals have been abundantly
preserved in Oregon, always in volcanic ash or
sedimentary layers. But fossils of such animals
are seldom found in Washington because any large
ash deposits are buried deep under many layers of
Columbia Plateau lava.
      But that lava created lakes by blocking stream
valleys, and preserved in those lake beds are fossil leaf impressions, petrified wood, fossil insects and bones of larger vertebrate animals. In
1984 an Ephrata man excavating the city landfill
found at the 30'-level an 18"-long bone fragment
that was part of a mammoth's 5-foot-long shoulder
bone. The Spokane flood probably carried it there.

3. LAVA PILLAR: Steins Pillar in Ochoco National Forest is one of Oregon's many unusual geological formations. The 350'-high rock, 120' in diameter, is a volcanic plug resembling the sturdy stem of a mushroom. 30 million years ago the area was buried by ash and lava from a volcanic eruption. Differential erosion left harder rock standing in a number of pillars. Steins is the largest.

4. BUTTE: A geological curiosity in Washington's Whitman County, Steptoe Butte was probably once a 9000' granite peak of the Selkirk Range. Now 3612' above sea level, rising 1200' above surrounding wheat fields, it is the largest "island" in the area. Floods of lava that buried smaller nearby peaks filled some valleys 6000' deep, but either did not reach the top of the ancient granite peak, or buried it until erosion exposed it.

Steptoe was an army officer whose 150 men were defeated in 1858 near the butte by 1000 Indians. Geologists use his name for such buttes.

5. BALANCED ROCK: One of Idaho's most unusual landmarks is Balanced Rock. The 40'-high, top-heavy rock resembles a huge stone mushroom as it balances on the edge of a bluff along Salmon Falls Creek Canyon. The base is only 1' x 1/2' x 3'. The granite rock rises above newer basalt.

6. CRATER: Hole-in-the-Ground Crater south of Mount Newberry in Oregon is a most unusual explosion crater several thousand feet in diameter. Rising several feet above the plain, it seems to be a meteorite hole. But its rim, almost a perfect circle, was formed of pyroclastic debris.

MIMA MOUNDS: *the most unusual and mysterious Northwest geological formation (Bob & Ira Spring)*

7. MOUNDS: Most unusual and mysterious in origin among the Northwest's geological formations are Washington's Mima Mounds. 900,000 once dotted an area of 30,000 acres. The Mima Mounds Natural Area protects about 4000 of the circular mounds, 1 to 7' high, and 10 to 40' in diameter. Inside, they are a random mix of clay, sand and pebbles on a coarse gravel-- building materials left behind by the retreating Vashon Glacier 15,000 years ago.

Similar mounds have been found at the limits of glaciation, but theories abound as to the origin of the Mima Mounds: buffalo mounds, Indian burial grounds, anthills, shellfish feast remains.

Two theories are current favorites. Either the mounds are glacial in origin, perhaps the result of repeated freezing and thawing; or they were made by ordinary pocket gophers, which create nesting mounds where hard soil or a high water table prevents burrowing. A family of the gophers can move 4 to 5 tons of earth a year. Seattle biologist Dr. Victor Scheffer found silt-filled cavities in the mounds that could be tunnels.

8. VOLCANIC CONE: The most unusual of Oregon's many volcanic cones is Fort Rock, amphitheatre-shaped remnant of an ancient tuff cone 325' high and 1/4 mile across, located in a state park south of Bend. The cone was built when hot magma rising to the surface came into contact with groundwater, causing steam explosions that ejected volcanic debris. Once, it was surrounded by a huge lake whose waves attacked the outer walls, collapsed the southwest side, and then battered the inner walls.

In a cave near the base of the rock was found evidence that prehistoric hunters used the cave--arrowheads and tools made of obsidian and agate (brought from the north). Sandals, 9000 years old, woven of sagebrush bark, were discovered in 1938 in Fort Rock Cave a mile west. At that time they were the oldest, directly dated artifacts of organic material of early man in the New World.

FORT ROCK: the most unusual of Oregon's many volcanic cones
(Oregon Dept. of Geology & Mineral Industries)

9. ERRATIC ROCK: Eastern Washington has an unusual balanced rock on a hillside on the Colville
Indian Reservation overlooking Omak Lake. It is
an erratic, transported far from its original site
by an Ice Age glacier. The slowly melting glacier
stranded the boulder, with soil between it and an
underlying rock. After the soil eroded away, the
erratic became a balanced rock.

*CITY OF ROCKS: Idaho's most unusual, historic rock formation in
some of North America's most ancient rock (Idaho Travel Council)*

10. ROCK CITY: Idaho's most unusual and historic
rock formation, formed from some of the world's
oldest rock, is the City of Rocks, 25 square miles
of rocks eroded by wind and weather from an enormous, isolated granite dome. The rocks look like
tubs, bottles, spires, turreted castles.

Below the "city" lies Emigrant Valley, where
Oregon and California wagon train routes split.
Wagon tracks are still visible in the soil. Emigrants camping nearby often cut names and dates
into the rocks or wrote them with axle grease.

11. CANYON: One of the Northwest's many unusual canyons, Crooked River Canyon near Prineville, is unique in having a canyon within a canyon. Much of the valley of the ancient Deschutes River and its tributaries was filled as deep as 700' with loose rock debris, through which the river cut a canyon. After lava 550' deep flowed down the canyon, the river eroded another channel in the lava. That inner canyon within the outer canyon can be clearly seen in many places.

Interesting, too, is one source of water for the river, which flows in an arid region with only 8 inches of rain a year. When irrigation water is withdrawn, the river may be dry near Prineville, but farther on, many warm springs issue from the stream bed and along the sides of the gorge. One of them, Opal Spring, washes opals to the surface.

THE ONLY

1. NICKEL MINE: The only major nickel mine now operating in the U.S., Hanna Nickel Mine, is located west of Riddle, Oregon, in Nickel Mountain. Nickel, essential in making iron alloys and steels that are heat- and chemical-resistant, is seldom found in deposits concentrated or accessible enough for profitable mining. Unable to compete with low-cost African nickel, Oregon's nickel is seldom mined without federal subsidies.

Hanna Mine, along with a dozen nearby smaller mines that operate sporadically, lies in a belt of serpentinite, a weak rock formed only in the lower part of bedrock sea floor. No other worthwhile nickel deposits have been found even though Oregon has abundant serpentinite, which contains such valuable minerals as platinum and chromite.

From prehistoric times, early humans made non-rusting tools from iron obtained from meteorites, whose iron contains 5 to 15 percent nickel.

2. **DRIFTWOOD BEACHES:** The world's only driftwood beaches are on the Pacific Northwest coast and on Puget Sound. Such beaches can occur only where an ample supply of timber grows near the water, as in Oregon and Washington, and where there are onshore winds, unique to the Northwest.

Although some driftwood floats in from distant points, most is of local origin. Many logs lost from log rafts in the Columbia River or in Puget Sound are carried out to sea and later washed up on ocean beaches. If roots are present, the tree was growing on a bank or a cliff at water's edge. Undermined by tidal action, the trees fall into the water. Since onshore winds push floating objects toward shore, the trees end up on the beach.

On East Coast beaches, which have offshore winds, only a few logs wash up. Oregon's choicest driftwood logs are Sitka spruce, myrtle (growing only in coastal counties) or any of three varieties of cedar, sand-polished to a satiny sheen.

DRIFTWOOD BEACHES: world's only driftwood beaches are on the Pacific Northwest coast (Saling)

3. VOLCANO SULPHUR: The only U.S. volcano on which sulphur was once mined is Mount Adams, Washington's second highest peak. Oldest Cascade volcano and most quiescent, it has extensive areas of sulphur-impregnated rock on its 210-acre summit plateau. As hydrogen sulphide gas passed through loose rocks on the crater floor and in surrounding areas, sulphur concentrated in the porous rocks. From 1932 to 1959 these were mined. Mules brought supplies and workers up, and sulphur down.

In July 1983 down its southwest slope roared the Northwest's largest avalanche in 25 years, a mile wide, containing a million cubic yards of ice, snow, rocks, and pumice. Mount Adams' east side has "glacier falls" so steep that the glacier is broken up into ice blocks.

THE MOST

1. FERTILE SOIL: The most fertile of all Northwest soil is Palouse loess of the richly productive Palouse Hills of eastern Washington and south western Idaho. The soil, 200' to 300' deep in places, is light, cohesive, fine-grained, uniform in texture, and almost free of rock fragments. It is not the result of lava weathering, but rather, wind-blown dust from glacial outwash deposits and old dunes; large deposits form downwind of such areas. They are thickest and most continuous in southeast Washington's rolling Palouse Hills, noted for wave-like contours and the nation's most productive wheat crops.

The fertile soil lies on top of basaltic lava in many high places throughout the Columbia Basin where the Spokane Floods did not scour it away. Wind-borne loess undoubtedly began to accumulate long after the Columbia Plateau lava flows but well before the end of the Ice Age. Winds were particularly strong during periods of glaciation when there was little vegetation to hold the soil.

2. THUNDEREGGS: Oregon has the nation's most thundereggs, that most sought-after of volcanic byproducts. Although not volcanic, the nodules form in volcanic rock and ash formations. The ugly, knobby exterior, sometimes as large as a grapefruit, conceals a center that may have beautiful crystals of quartz or calcite, and agate often banded or splashed with color. Weird or beautiful designs resemble trees, mushrooms, green moss, mountains, golden plumes. Each is unique.

Thundereggs are found in arid central and southeastern Oregon, especially around Prineville and east of Madras. Ledges of partially welded ash in John Day Formation have yielded thousands.

The angular cavities may require millions of years to fill with agate or crystals as silica is slowly precipitated by groundwater. More millions of years pass before weathering exposes the eggs.

3. WESTERLY LAND: Washington has the lower 48's most westerly and most northwesterly points of land. Most northwesterly is Cape Flattery at the tip of the Olympic Peninsula; most westerly by a few hundred feet is Cape Alava, 15 miles south.

Cape Alava, occupied by Makah Indians for several thousand years, was the site of the Ozette Village Archeological Excavation. Thousands of artifacts were recovered from 500-year-old Makah homes flattened and sealed by mudslides.

At Cape Flattery a rough half-mile trail leads to Land's End Lookout, with a view of sheer cliffs and battered rocks on both sides of the cape. Offshore, Tatoosh Island lighthouse is one of the Northwest's oldest, built near the entrance to the Strait of Juan de Fuca in 1857.

TATOOSH ISLAND LIGHTHOUSE: one of Northwest's oldest, off Cape Flattery, lower 48's northwesternmost point (U.S. Coast Guard)

4. SNOW: The most snow ever accumulated in one spot in a year-- 93'-- piled up at Paradise Ranger Station at Mount Rainier, Feb. 19, 1971 to Feb. 18, 1972. That area, at 5500' elevation, also holds a world record for the greatest depth of snow in a single month: 25',5" in April 1972. Snowfall is heavier farther up the mountain, but tapers off at about 10,000', since very cold air holds less moisture, and the mountain top is often above storms. Weather on its upper slopes can exceed that of Everest, with minus-55° F. and 100 mph winds. White-outs, not rare, are dangerous.

The winter of 1861-62 was so cold that the steamer Multnomah was frozen in ice along the Columbia River shore near Cathlamet.

5. RAIN: The most rain on record that has ever fallen in one year in the lower 48-- 184.56"-- drenched the community of Wynooche-Oxbow 25 miles northeast of Aberdeen, Washington, in 1933. Rain can last for days there, thick mist for weeks. The Quinault Rain Forest averages 134" a year. Mount Olympus receives even more precipitation than Wynoochie-Oxbow-- 200" each year-- but most of that is snow. On Jan. 21, 1935, 12" of rain fell in 24 hours at the ranger station there. In any winter month in the rain forest, 40" of rain can fall. Yet 40 miles away, Sequim has only 17", the driest coastal region north of San Diego.

The Olympic Peninsula receives so much rain because of moisture-laden clouds sweeping in from the Pacific, and because the winds, in rising to clear the high Olympic Mountains, become chilled, and thus, less able to hold moisture. So they dump rain abundantly on the Olympic slopes blocking their way. Little moisture is left as the clouds pass the eastern, rain-shadow side of the Olympics, and Sequim. But moisture builds up as winds reach the Cascades and rise again. The clouds are fairly dry when they reach Idaho.

6. MOUNTAIN RANGES: Idaho has the most mountain ranges in the Northwest with 22 distinct ranges, 8 of them major. With 9/10 of its surface covered by mountains, it may be the most mountainous, in relation to total area, of any lower-48 state.

Mountains run along Idaho's eastern boundary from Canada to the southeastern tip where it meets Utah and Wyoming. The Bitterroot Range forms more than half of the uneven Idaho-Montana boundary.

Its Centennial Mountains are one of the few U.S. mountain ranges running east and west. Some of the most outstanding mountain groups are the Seven Devils, rising above Hells Canyon; the jagged Sawtooths, youngest range of the Rockies and often considered the most spectacular mountains in the Northwest; the Lost River Range, Idaho's highest mountains, with Mount Borah at 12,665'. 200 of Idaho's peaks are over 8000' high; 18 are over 11,000'; 7, over 12,000'.

BITTERROOT MOUNTAINS-- one of many mountain ranges in Idaho-- Northwest's most mountainous state (Idaho Travel Council)

THE MOST RECENT

1. MOUNTAINS: Among North America's most recently created mountains are Washington's Olympics. They were probably uplifted in the same crustal upheavals that created the modern Cascades.

The Cascades are linear; the Olympic Mountains are a broad and massive dome deeply eroded down all sides by glaciation. Despite their youth, they contain some of North America's oldest rock, uplifted from the sea. But no Olympic peak is volcanic. The mountains were once thought to have a granite core, however, because many massive granite boulders are found in Olympic Peninsula rivers and on slopes as high as 3000'. But those boulders are erratics, rafted in ice from British Columbia during several ice ages. Any lava present is basaltic-- breccia, volcanic tuff, pillow basalt (whose rounded forms indicate underwater eruption). These volcanic rocks are often found as outcroppings on exposed Olympic Mountain slopes.

The Olympic Mountains are an outstanding example of the results of continental drift, of the collision between the Juan De Fuca oceanic plate and the North American continental plate. Their primary building materials were river-deposited sand and silt, later metamorphosed by intense heat and pressure into sandstone. These materials may have been shoved into an oceanic trough on a subsiding sea floor by the collision of the two plates. Later, the chaotic mass was uplifted into the jumble of crags and folds that are the Olympic Mountains, with some sections tilted 90°. The chaos makes geological conclusions difficult.

As the uplift continued, streams originating at the highest peaks in the center of the dome flowed down in every direction, cutting ridges and valleys. These were later scoured even deeper by ice age alpine glaciers which were much larger than today's sixty glaciers and extended lower.

The present rivers, all originating in glacial cirques and fed by snow- and glacier-melt, still flow down all sides of the domed range in a radial pattern of drainage. As they follow glacial valleys, they cut their own inner gorges 100 feet deep. Five major rivers flow down the gentler west side: Bogachiel, Queets, Hoh, Quinault, and Soleduck. The Hoh receives 80% of the drainage from Mount Olympus, highest Olympic peak at 7965 feet. Six glaciers wrap around two-thirds of it; largest are the Blue and the Hoh.

Meltwater from many small glaciers and snow-fields on the north sides of the highest peaks feeds rivers such as the Elwha and Dungeness, which flow into the Strait of Juan de Fuca.

The Olympics are divided into two climatic zones. The abrupt relief on the windward side causes the heaviest precipitation in the lower 48, 140" on the coast, 40' of snow on high peaks.

OLYMPIC MOUNTAINS: a view from Hurricane Ridge of some of North America's most recently created mountains (Saling)

2. LAVA FIELDS: The most recent large lava flow
in the lower 48 is Jordan Craters Lava Flow, only
500 years old, 4 by 30 miles. Another large flow
is the McKenzie Lavafields, 70 square miles of
jumbled lava with some so recent, 1500 years old,
that nothing grows on it. The lava flowed from
Belknap Crater, South Belknap and Little Belknap.
    Only Idaho's Craters of the Moon, a bit larg-
er and older, is as impressive. The old McKenzie
Pass Highway cuts through a wilderness of lava,
crossing Oregon's highest east-west mountain pass,
5324'. Sometimes 6 miles wide, the basalt flowed
for 12 miles, moving into the canyon of the McKenzie River, altering the river's course. Today's
McKenzie River disappears into permeable sediments
along the flow margins, runs underground and then
reappears at Tamolitch Falls.

3. VOLCANIC ERUPTION: The most recent volcanic
eruption in the lower 48, the largest in U.S. history and the first since 1917, one of the most
powerful explosions witnessed by humans (500 times
the force of Hiroshima's) burst from Washington's
Mount St. Helens, one of the youngest Cascade volcanoes, on May 18, 1980 at 8:31 a.m. The nation's
most dangerous volcano, it was still the only
active volcano in the lower 48 in 1986.
    After 123 years of dormancy and months of
warnings-- the bulging north side grew 5 feet a
day-- the volcano exploded so violently that it
reduced its symmetrical summit cone 1313', from
9677' to 8364'. It dropped at once from fifth
highest mountain in Washington to thirtieth.
    The main event started with an earthquake (5.1
on the Richter scale). Fifteen seconds later the
bulge, now 330' high, blew out with a shock wave
heard 225 miles away in Vancouver, B.C. The release of pressure within the volcano triggered an
explosion of steam and gases that hurled rock debris through the breach in the north side.

The unholy trinity of heat, wind and debris worked together. That first blast sent an avalanche of huge blocks of ice and snow racing down the slopes. The heat of the explosion melted glacial ice and snow, which mixed with soil to become a mudslide (at 900° F.). It swept down at 250 mph, picking up debris and catching the avalanche.

The blast of scorching air vastly increased the range of damage, burned, knocked down, uprooted huge trees 15 to 30 miles away. Spirit Lake was clogged with debris. 26 lakes were destroyed, 27 damaged, and 298 miles of rivers and streams. Debris, blown from the bulge and from a fractured summit crater, and picked up by avalanche and mudflow, overwhelmed forests and rivers. The pulverized mountain dumped 600,000 tons of ash on Yakima, 85 miles to the east, darkening the sky. All day heat-lightning streaked the purplish clouds of ash and pulverized rock suspended in volcanic gases. The clouds soared upward 63,000', circling the globe.

Most surprising was the destructive lateral force. More than 150 square miles of forest were leveled, including 60,000 acres of 200'-high Douglas firs. 57 people were dead or missing, perhaps 1.5 million animals killed.

Mount St. Helens is now the most studied volcano in the world, with temperature probes in steam vents and seismic monitors on crater dome and mountain. The giant is sleeping fitfully.

THE MOST VARIED

1. PETRIFIED TREES: Washington's Ginkgo Petrified Forest has the most varied species of trees
of any petrified forest in the world. More than
200 species have been identified there. These
include many water- or moisture-loving species
that no longer grow in the Pacific Northwest. Before the Cascades rose and cut off the moist ocean
air, the climate in eastern Washington was often
warm and moist in the long intervals between lava
flows. Lakes and swamps were abundant; tropical
shrubs and trees flourished.

Among the trees petrified during that period,
when highly liquid basaltic lava flooded the Columbia Basin again and again, were hemlock, Douglas
fir, pine, spruce, crabapple, hickory, gum, birch,
myrtle, ash, buckeye, magnolia, cypress, chestnut,
sycamore, 3 species of elm, 9 of oak, 8 of walnut,
10 of maple. Sequoias reached 10 feet in diameter,
and ginkgo thrived, one of the most ancient trees,
now believed not to grow wild anywhere.

Ginkgo leaves are often found fossilized but
the wood, rarely. At the forest site, ginkgo
seeds, leaves, limbs and trunks fell from hills
into the lowland swamps and lakes. Any trees
found with bark and roots probably fell where they
grew, unbattered by stream transport. Those petrified without bark and branches probably floated
down the river and stranded in the silt of swamps
and deltas. Some were found at an angle, as if
they had been in a log jam.

This petrified forest is unusual because the
trees were not burned up by the engulfing lava.
They were preserved because they were waterlogged,
and because the lava that entered the water where
they lay, cooled so rapidly that it formed pillow
basalt around the water-soaked, sediment-buried
trees. Later flows buried them deep.

Over the centuries the logs were petrified by

groundwater containing silica, seeping through the
lava and penetrating the buried logs. Opal and
chalcedony, forms of silica, were precipitated in
the logs, replacing cellulose, preserving even
growth rings. The brilliant colors and strange
designs in the petrified wood were caused by iron,
manganese and other minerals in the groundwater.
    The process occurred over millions of years.
The large size of the trees and great variety tes-
tify to the long periods between the devastating
lava flows -- time for new soil to form and large
trees to grow again. Among them is a maple 50'
high, an oak 6' in diameter, a spruce 100' high.
    After the Cascades were uplifted, the area
became dry. Eventually erosion by ice and by
floods cut through the many layers of lava,
exposing the petrified trees. Many successive
layers of petrified trees may still be buried.

2. **GEMSTONES:** Idaho has the most varied assortment of gemstones in the Northwest-- more than 80
varieties. Almost every county in "The Gem State"
has gemstones. Many of the creeks where they are
found are so remote that very little collecting
has been done in them. Most of Idaho's old ghost
towns have interesting rocks and gemstones.

Idaho is the only place in North America where
there are enough fire opals to mine commercially.
Turn-of-the-century opals found there equalled in
color any opals in the world. Even fossil bones
in Owyhee County are sometimes encrusted with fire
opal. Garnets and emeralds can be found in the
north. In the mountain lakes region there are
sapphires. Central Idaho has diamonds (poor quality), rubies, aquamarines, and garnets in six
colors. Found in the tremendous lava flows that
formed the Snake River Plains in the south are
agate and agatized wood, jasper and opal.

At Graveyard Point, agate is found in veins a
foot wide with plumes of white, red, yellow and
blue. At Beacon Hill west of Weiser, nodules are
filled with blue agate and green moss agate, and
geodes lined with amethyst. Emerald Creek near
Clarkia has dark purple or plum-colored star garnets, Idaho's state gemstone, more precious than
star rubies or star sapphires. Also found are
beryl, zircon, malachite, topaz, and tourmaline.

3. **LAVA FORMATIONS:** North America's most varied
lava formations are found in Oregon and in Idaho.
High Lava Plains, a high cool plateau in Oregon's
Deschutes National Forest, has one of the continent's best concentrations of varied volcanic
landforms. These include Lava Butte, the world's
largest cinder cone, most accessible of all Cascade cones, 500' high with a road to the top;
Oregon's longest lava tube cave, 6700'-long Lava
River Tunnel; lava ice caves; Lava Cast Forest,
one of the world's largest; Newberry Crater, one

of the largest calderas in the world, containing
two lakes and several obsidian flows. Mount Newberry sits on top of huge Brothers Fault.

Newberry provided nine miles of lava, 6000
years ago, that inundated a living forest of
pines, now Lava Cast Forest. Some of the trees
are upright "stone trees"-- hollow lava tubes
rising above the surface of the flow. Others were
knocked over and are pipe-like casts, some 20 feet
long, one 2½ feet in diameter.

Most trees burn up when covered with hot lava,
but some are buried in lava that cools upon contact with the moist wood; a thin crust of lava
hardens around the tree trunk, preserving even the
bark imprint. Cooler lava may only char the wood,
which then rots, leaving a mold.

Newberry also spewed out the lava in which
Lava River Caves are located. Some have lavacicles
and "bathtub rings" that show previous levels of
lava flowing through the tube before it emptied
out. Some former lava tubes whose roofs collapsed
now form steep-sided valleys 40 to 50 feet high.

Lava that covered 10 square miles poured from
the base of Lava Butte, a well-preserved, extinct
cone whose crater is 150' deep. That lava dammed
the Deschutes River, forcing it to cut a new channel around the flow, with rapids and waterfalls.

At the northeast corner of the Snake River
Plains at 7576' elevation, in one of the world's
most extensive lava flows, Idaho's Craters of the
Moon National Monument displays in 83 square miles
more basaltic volcanic features than any other
area its size in the lower 48. It is part of a
much larger lava field.

There are 63 craters, 100 fumaroles, 9 lava
tree molds, 17 main lava caves (2 are 30' in diameter), 4 natural bridges, (one 125' long), 19
prominent cinder cones, lava bombs of every shape
and size, and Big Cinder Butte, 800' high, the
world's largest purely basaltic cinder cone.

Most of the lava flows were quiet, issuing
from fissures. But giant trees toppled into the

lava and some were preserved. One unusual formation is a cobalt-blue flow of "squeeze-up" lava.
Largest lava cave is Indian Cave.

The Monument includes some of the nation's
most recent lava flows, 1600 years old. But all
the lava looks much younger than it is. With
rainfall of only 10" a year, erosion is minimal.

Craters of the Moon spatter cones are the best
examples of this type of formation in the lower
48. They formed from fountains spouting pasty
lava; clots stuck together, falling back near the
vent. Symmetrical cinder cones also formed from
lava fountains, but with gas-filled lava that
cooled and hardened into cinders while falling
around the vent.

Wagon trains and stage coaches knew the area
and used it as a landmark, but they avoided it
even though it was a shorter route.

*CRATERS OF THE MOON: a lava tree cast is among most varied
lava formations in North America (Idaho Travel Council)*

THE RICHEST

1. GOLD AND SILVER: Idaho had the richest deposits of gold and silver ever found in the U.S. The single richest find in the U.S. within 18 square miles was in Placerville and Quartzburg in Boise National Forest. Idaho City alone produced more gold than Alaska. Most of the ore deposits contact the huge Idaho Batholith. Oregon's major ore deposits in the Blue and Wallowa Mountains were also associated with batholiths, which are probably offshoots of Idaho's.

Since 1884 Coeur d'Alene Mining District, one of the world's richest mining areas and largest silver producer in terms of total historical production, has produced metals worth $2 billion, 3/4 of Idaho's total. That district, a 20-mile area between Kellogg and Mullan within the canyon of the South Fork of the Coeur d'Alene River, includes the nation's largest producing silver mine, Idaho's Sunshine Mine, one of the oldest in the valley. The 5000'-deep mine outproduced the Comstock Lode all by itself.

From 1860-1960, mineral production in Idaho totaled $2.5 billion, with $950 million in lead and $537 million in silver, double the production of Nevada's Comstock Lode. Lead, zinc, copper and antimony are byproducts of silver mining.

Gold was first discovered in 1860, with richer sources found in 1862, much of it in quartz veins. The greatest strike was in 1884 when silver, lead and zinc were found in the Coeur d'Alene district. More lead and silver were mined there in 1886-8 than had ever before been found in one place.

Until those discoveries, Idaho had been thinly settled, an arid place to pass through on the way to Oregon. But discovery of gold and silver lured thousands of people, and in 1863 Idaho was made a separate territory, and in 1898, a state. Boundaries were drawn to include all the new mines.

2. **FOSSILS:** The richest concentration of prehistoric mammalian fossils in the U.S. was discovered
in Oregon's John Day fossil beds in 1861. Famous
the world over, the formations, many of them included in the John Day Fossil Beds National Monument, have attracted paleontologists and students
from many countries. There they can study evolution in certain species over millions of years.
There are nearly continuous fossil records for 60
million years during the Age of Mammals.

John Day Canyon, 1500' deep and almost unequaled in the world for rugged beauty as well as
fossils, is almost unrivaled in its cross-section
display of eight past geological epochs. The age
of the rocks in the oldest, lowest layer is not
known, but they reveal ancient flora and fauna.
Upon them lies mud hardened into rock containing
marine fossils from the sea that once covered the
area. Next come sand and gravel older than the
Alps, Rockies and Himalayas, also with fossils.

After that are deep lava flows, and then, some
of the Northwest's most beautifully colored volcanic ash in a sequence continuous for 7 million
years. The lower layer is brown, the middle layer
green, the top a pale yellow-brown.

That colorful ash was erupted with great vio-
lence some 30 million years ago from new volcanoes
in the western Cascades that sent huge clouds of
light-colored ash over central Oregon. The ash is
more than 1000' deep in the John Day Formation.
Animals whose fossilized bones have been found in
the area were smothered by the ash that filled
lake beds and choked streams.

On top of the ash are the great Columbia Plateau lava flows. Ashy strata are last, with coarse
gravel and volcanic tufa. Most of the rock is
rather soft, made of wind-carried ash, but there
are some unusual ledges of very hard rock-- volcanic ash welded into a solid mass. Similar welded ash ledges cover thousands of square miles from
western Canada to south of Salem. There has been

no other volcanic eruption so enormous known to
have occurred in historic times. And none has
produced welded ash beds more than a few miles
from the vent, or covered more than a few miles.
  John Day Fossil Beds National Monument is made
up of three widely separated units. Largest is
Sheep Rock, named for an impressive, basalt-capped
landmark with buff and red layers. The unit runs
for 7 miles along the river that winds through
Picture Gorge, cut through high basalt cliffs.
Walls of the narrow canyon reveal red tropical
soil contrasting with layers of black basalt.
  Unit 2 is domed Painted Hills, famous for its
colorful landscape, and the lava flows of Picture

*JOHN DAY FOSSIL BEDS NATIONAL MONUMENT: lava-capped Sheep Rock in
nation's richest concentration of prehistoric mammalian fossils
(Oregon Economic Development Dept.)*

Gorge basalt. The hills and ridges are pink, red, bronze, gold and charcoal.

Clarno, the northernmost unit, is noted for palisades and pinnacles of bronze-colored rock, and its Plant Fossil Beds. It is one of the few places in the world where fossil plants are preserved with seeds, leaves, stems in the same location. Some of the plants species survive today: walnut, grape, palm, pistachio, water lily.

Fossilized leaves and seeds in the middle and upper ash layers reveal a drastically different climate in that part of Oregon 30 million years ago -- warm, moist, with lush vegetation and subtropical forests with flowering trees. Leaf imprints have been found of palm, ginkgo, magnolia, avocado, cinnamon and fig trees.

Animal species in Oregon at that time included mammoths, crocodiles, flamingos, camels, rhinos, giant pigs, 3-toed horses, giant sloths, tapirs, bison, turtles, and saber-toothed tigers. Fragmented bones of many have been found at John Day.

THE LARGEST

1. ISLAND: Whidbey Island, 50 miles long, is the largest U.S. island in Puget Sound, and the longest of the lower 48. In 1985 the U.S. Supreme Court decided that Long Island was not an island but a peninsula. That made Whidbey Number One.

The northern half lies in the lee of the Olympic rain shadow and is so dry that cactus grow naturally in some places. The climate of the south end matches Seattle's. The island has headlands, forests, and beaches with the largest sanddunes found on Puget Sound. Along its coves and inlets are three incorporated cities.

Coupeville, founded in 1853, is one of Washington's oldest towns. Its oldest home is that of Captain Coupe (1853).

2. MUDFLOW: 5800 years ago one of the largest, most catastrophic mudflows known to have occurred, the Osceola Mudflow, lowered by nearly 2000 feet Mount Rainier, the Northwest's highest mountain. Before the mudflow, Mount Rainier towered almost 16,000 feet high.

Mudflows often accompany an eruption, as they did on Mount St. Helens, causing vast destruction. The total volume of the Osceola Mudflow was more than half a cubic mile. The material in it was rock at and under the volcano summit that had been chemically converted to clay minerals by gases and heat flowing from crater steam vents. Rain and groundwater seeped into the soil, became heated, and then rose through vents to convert the rock.

Even without a triggering force, such soft rock is susceptible to erosion or sliding. This flow, however, was triggered by violent steam explosions. The summit collapsed, providing ample material for the mudflow. One section of the flow raced down Emmons Glacier, largest glacier in the lower 48 today. The wall of rock and mud was 500' high when it passed the present White River campground. Another lobe descended Winthrop Glacier into the West Fork of the White River. The two lobes then joined, extending 65 miles, burying 125 square miles of lowlands. The flow leveled the landscape by filling in lowland valleys, inundating the present sites of Auburn, Kent, Enumclaw, Sumner, and Puyallup. Part of it reached Puget Sound at Commencement Bay.

After the mudflow, the summit crater was a caldera nearly 2 miles in diameter, with the highest points on its wall the same as today's: Liberty Cap, 14,112', and Point Success, 14,150'.

Later lava flows, relatively recent, built a new cone on the old base, filling most of the caldera created by the collapse, and making the mountain more symmetrical. Still later, east of the older vent, lava eruptions formed a larger crater 1300' across and 500' deep. The present highest point of Mount Rainier, Columbia Crest, 14,410 feet, rises where the two craters overlap.

There were human witnesses to the Osceola Mudflow. Excavation turned up the oldest dated human tools yet found in the Puget Sound area, more than 200 projectile points, scrapers, and drills, buried under mudflow debris near Enumclaw.

With steam jets in its craters today, and a ground temperature of 174 degrees F. near the vents, Mount Rainier is still prone to mudflows. Two large ones have occurred in this century.

3. PHOSPHATE: Idaho has the world's largest reserve of phosphate, 268,000 acres, 1/3 of all the phosphate known in North America. It is located near Montpelier and Soda Springs at 5779' near highly mineralized hot springs. Phosphate is used in sulfuric acid, fertilizers and phosphoric acid.

4. LAVA CAVE LAKE: Malheur Cave, a lava tube cave in Oregon, has within it North America's largest permanent lake located in a lava cave, where lakes are rarely found. The lake varies in size seasonally, up to 2000' long and 25' wide, the width of the lava tube. At its lower end, the lake is 23' deep. The water is a mixture of thermal spring and regional groundwater. The lake contains animal life-- two crustaceans, a flatworm, and an subterranean pseudo-scorpion.

5. ISLAND: Largest island off the Northwest coast is Washington's Destruction Island, 3½ miles out. The long-time navigational landmark is the first island north of the Farallons. It was the scene of two historic Indian massacres. Killed were crew members of two sailing ships, six sent ashore from a Spanish ship in 1775, and seven from an English ship in 1787.

6. SEA CAVE: Oregon's Sea Lion Caves are North America's largest natural sea cave. Located midway on the Oregon coast north of Florence, the cave is the only mainland breeding and wintering home for a herd of about 200 Steller's (northern) sea lions, largest of the sea lions. Other sea lions breed and winter on offshore rocks.

The sea-level cave was excavated by wave action exploiting faults and a soft sedimentary layer below the hard basalt of a 300-foot-high lava headland. It was discovered in 1880 by a man who rowed a small boat inside. The main chamber is 125' high and 500' in diameter, with two acres of always-flooded floor space. Moss and algae color ceilings green, pink, red and purple.

There are three natural openings. A 1000-foot-long corridor is dry at low tide. Through another shorter one, the ocean washes in constantly with enough force to carry the sea lions inside and up onto the rocks. A third entrance, fifty feet above the ocean, serves as an observation area.

SEA LION CAVES: North America's largest natural sea cave, on scenic Oregon Coast (Sea Lion Caves Inc.)

7. CALDERA: Oregon's Newberry Volcano, one of the largest Ice Age volcanoes, has one of the world's largest calderas, 3 by 4 miles, with walls 1500' high. Before its summit collapsed, this was Oregon's highest shield volcano, 10,000' high. Highest point today is Paulina Peak, 7985'.

Within the caldera are two lakes; several huge obsidian flows, one of them among the world's most extensive; and cinder cones atop lava flows. Central Pumice Cone, 1 mile wide, 700' high, has a 250-foot-deep crater. From a high vent, a frozen cataract of obsidian descends to the crater floor.

Cinder cones separate two deep-blue caldera lakes, once a single lake. East Lake, higher than Paulina Lake and lacking an outlet, is fed by hot mineral springs. Paulina Creek, outlet for Paulina Lake, has cut through the caldera walls.

MOUNT NEWBERRY CRATER: one of the world's largest calderas with 2 lakes and one of world's largest obsidian flows inside it (Oregon Dept. of Geology & Mineral Industries)

Newberry's quiet, very liquid flows traveled for miles. The summit collapse was not the result of violent eruptions but rather, great flows from more than 200 cinder cones dotting the gentle outer slopes. Cones range from 200 to 500' high, between ¼ and ½ mile in diameter, with craters up to 300' deep. Newberry straddles Brothers Fault, one of the continent's largest exposed faults.

Newberry lava engulfed a living forest to form perhaps the world's largest lava cast forest. Many lava tube caves were formed in its lava.

Newberry's volcanic activity both predates and postdates Mount Mazama's. Mazama ash 10 to 20" deep tops Newberry flows, and is, in turn, topped by Newberry lava. The volcano has ejected four kinds of lava, possibly from different magma chambers at different levels.

8. METEORITE: The largest meteorite ever found in the U.S., the Willamette Meteorite, was discovered in Oregon in 1902 by a woodcutter. Even with several pieces broken off by scientists, it weighs 13.5 tons. Somehow, the woodcutter dug out the cone-shaped, embedded meteorite and winched it into a home-made wagon. It took him three months to haul it 3/4 of a mile by horse and wagon to his own land, over steep hillsides and through a forested canyon. He built a shed over his find and charged 25 cents to see the meteorite.

Oregon Iron and Steel, owners of the land on which the meteorite had been found, sued to get it back, and won. The meteorite was exhibited at the 1905 Lewis and Clark Centennial Fair in Portland, and eventually wound up at the Hayden Planetarium.

Local Indians called the meteorite a "visitor from the moon." Before battles, Indian warriors dipped arrowheads into rainwater that collected in pits on the meteorite.

In 1856 a geologist on a government survey near Port Orford, Oregon, found a meteorite almost

WILLAMETTE METEORITE: largest ever found in the U.S., more than 13.4 tons (Oregon Historical Society)

as large; he estimated it at 10 tons. A piece of it was among rocks he sent to the Smithsonian Institute, but it was not identified until 1859. Although, according to the geologist, 5 or 6 feet of the meteorite projected from the ground in a treeless, rockless area, with Bald Mountain as a landmark, the meteorite has never been seen again.

9. PUMICE: The largest amount of pumice ejected in some of the most violent eruptions of any recent Cascade volcano came from Mount Mazama. It may have been Oregon's highest volcano 6845 years ago, about 12,000', before its summit collapsed.

Thousands of years before those explosions, the volcano erupted out huge amounts of pumice, formed from dacite lava, a very stiff lava often causing violent eruptions. Glowing avalanches of superheated pumice and other debris deposited deep layers of welded tuff.

Other eruptions of thick andesite lava from the volcano's flanks piled up 600 feet deep to form the Watchman, now prominent on the caldera rim, and a large cone whose remains form Hillman Peak, 2000 feet above Crater Lake. After a period of glaciation, a new dacite flow 1200 feet deep filled a glaciated valley, exposed as Llao Rock on the rim after the summit collapse. Meanwhile, two dozen cones forming near the base probably drained off enough magma to help cause the collapse.

Other violent eruptions of pumice occurred, more glowing avalanches, a final glacial period, and a quiet interval during which forests grew on the mountain's slopes. Then came the final eruptions. Huge explosions of frothy pumice deposited wind-carried ash over hundreds of thousands of miles to the northeast. Pumice boulders six feet in diameter were found 20 miles from the crater.

Glowing avalanches raced down the mountain at 100 mph. One crossed Diamond Lake and continued beyond it. Glowing avalanches flowing east had enough momentum to travel 25 miles across flat land. Canyons near the volcano were filled to depths of 250 feet or more.

As the hot lava, 300 feet deep in places, slowly cooled, emerging gases forced their way through the deposits, forming vents as high as 200 feet. The heat cemented the scoria and pumice of the vents, hardening them. Later erosion of the softer pumice left spire-like pinnacles clustered in nearby canyons.

Pumice or volcanic ash from those eruptions covered 350,000 square miles. Mazama Ash is found in Oregon, Washington, Idaho, Wyoming, Montana, northeastern California, northern Nevada, southern British Columbia, and southwestern Alberta.

In its final days Mount Mazama may have blown out 42 cubic miles of pyroclastic material, formed from 16 cubic miles of liquid magma, which greatly expands when discharged as pumice. Without the magma chamber to help support the weight of the top, the summit was undermined and collapsed, creating one of the world's largest calderas, 5 by 6 miles wide, nearly 4000 feet deep with a high point of 8156 feet.

Later flows leveled the crater floor and built several cinder cones, some now under water. Many years passed before the caldera was cool enough for Crater Lake to form within it.

Artifacts buried in the ash suggest that pre-historic inhabitants died during the final eruptions. Fish must have been killed in ash-clogged rivers and streams, as they were by the Mount St. Helens eruption, for Stone Age Indians at that time changed their diet from salmon to big game.

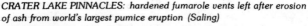

CRATER LAKE PINNACLES: hardened fumarole vents left after erosion of ash from world's largest pumice eruption (Saling)

10. WATERFALL: The world's largest waterfall,
Washington's Dry Falls, was created almost entirely by repetitions of the Spokane Floods, greatest
floods known in the world. Water plunged over 3
deeply notched, horseshoe-shaped cliffs in lower
Grand Coulee. They are 3½ miles across the crest
and 400' high. The only water there now is in
plunge pools at the base, but millions of years
ago, torrents of water roared over the cliffs.

Enormous amounts of flood water during an unknown number of Spokane Floods rushed into what
was probably already a shallow gorge, deepened by
a Columbia River swollen with glacial meltwater.
The river was diverted from its normal channel by
thousands of feet of glacial ice that buried the
Okanogan Valley near today's Grand Coulee Dam.

The lip of the falls, formed of easily eroded,
cracked basaltic lava, was constantly chewed away
by the rush of rock-filled water. Erosion caused
the great cataract to retreat quickly upstream
from Soap Lake, leaving behind a deep coulee more
than 20 miles long. During the height of flooding, the chasm was hidden by water flowing well
above its rim, but the scouring action continued.

The coulee, dry between floods, must have been
deepened by each successive flood. Each flood
may have lasted only a few weeks while Glacial
Lake Missoula emptied out after the breaching of
its ice dam. But those brief periods were enough
to cut Dry Falls and the other coulees that vein
eastern Washington.

11. COULEE: Washington's Grand Coulee is one of
the world's largest coulees and one of the world's
most impressive examples of glacial and flood
drainage. Really two coulees at different levels
joined by Dry Falls, the chasm runs southwest for
52 miles. Upper Grand Coulee, 27 miles long, is
often 4 miles wide and 900' deep. Probably once a
shallow valley, the chasm was gradually enlarged

by a Columbia River diverted from its channel by a thick sheet of glacial ice, and much enlarged by glacier-melt. Long after the glacier had melted and the Columbia resumed its normal course, abandoning the coulees and other alternative channels, enormous amounts of flood water poured over the area, filling the dry coulees with torrents of rock-laden water. The same floods that carved out Dry Falls gouged out this deeper, wider coulee.

After the final flood, Grand Coulee was dry until Grand Coulee Dam was built. Then, water was stored in the Coulee for irrigation use.

DRY FALLS: world's largest waterfall ever, 3 1/2 miles across, 400' deep, caused by world's greatest floods (Saling)

12. FLOOD: The world's largest flood, really as many as 40 repetitions of the Spokane Flood, was responsible for most of the distinctive topographical features of eastern Washington. The floods resulted from repeated blocking by thick lobes of glacial ice of Idaho's Clark Fork River near Lake

Pend Oreille. Each time, the river backed up into western Montana, forming Glacial Lake Missoula behind an ice dam, 1000 to 2000 feet high. Time after time the dam was breached, and ice-clogged flood waters rushed into eastern Washington across Idaho's narrow Panhandle.

The maximum height of the 300-square-mile lake is marked on cliffs bordering it-- 2000'. Whenever the dam gave way, a towering wall of water must have surged out of the lake, requiring several weeks, perhaps a month, for the 500 cubic miles of water to empty. Even 200 to 300 miles away, the flood waters were at least 700' high. At the site of Grand Coulee Dam, they were perhaps 2500' deep, 1200' higher than today's dam.

Since river channels could not handle so much water in the lava-leveled Basin, it spilled out onto the Columbia Plateau near Spokane, flowing west and southwest. Best known of the hundreds of coulees and canyons scoured out by the flood are Grand Coulee, Moses Coulee, and Dry Falls.

Wherever the water passed, the plateau was swept clean of its thick covering of wind-borne loess. Although flood waters extended into northern Willamette Valley, and created a lake 400' deep south of Portland, only eastern Washington was so devastatingly eroded. Channeled scablands are found only there, formed as flood water cut through huge hills of fine dust. Higher peaks were spared, especially in the Palouse Hills. There, the floods created a 40-mile-long series of basaltic "islands," each capped with its deep loess, separated from each other by channels gouged down to basalt bedrock. Those fertile islands now produce prolific crops.

The water backed up to create lakes, some permanent, others temporary. The largest was behind Wallula Gap, a narrow channel with sheer cliffs eroded by the Columbia through Horse Heaven Hills basalt. Here, flood water drained into the Columbia Gorge, scouring the lower walls down to bare rock and undercutting walls on the Oregon side, creating the sheer cliffs over which water-falls now plunge. The high gorge walls channeled the flood water out into the ocean.

The realization that repeated floods of such magnitude had carved the coulees and scablands came only in the 1960s after long insistence by J. H. Bretz. The evidence is overwhelming, spread over 2900 square miles. Large deposits of gravel and sand, often marked with giant ripples more than 10 feet high with hundreds of feet between crests, are found in the Pasco Basin along the Columbia River. Huge boulders torn from fractured basalt are scattered over the Plateau. Icebergs of glacial ice rafted in flood water contained great rocks, usually granite and gneiss from the north. These erratics are found from the Grand Coulee Dam area down to the Pasco Basin, even in the Willamette Valley, 100 miles south of the glacial margins. East of the Cascades they were deposited at elevations up to 1100 feet.

The flood changed the course of the Palouse River so that it emptied into the Snake River, not directly into the Columbia, as before. Palouse Canyon was created as Palouse Falls, 185' high, eroded away the lip of its cliff, retreating up-stream more than seven miles, cutting a canyon 400 to 800 feet deep in a very short time.

Idaho's Snake River Canyon was also deepened by great floods from an ancient glacial lake, 20,000-square-mile Lake Bonneville, largest ever in North America. Great Salt Lake is the only surviving remnant of this lake, which overflowed and rushed through a high pass near Pocatello. So much water spilled into the Snake's deep canyon that it too overflowed. The flood waters tore boulders from the slopes of the canyon walls and tumbled them along until they grounded in Hells Canyon. Flood waters in Washington also carried extraordinarily large boulders. But everything about the floods was extraordinary.

PART FOUR

THE HUMAN WORLD

THE DEEPEST

MINE: One of North America's deepest mine shafts
was completed in 1983 at the Lucky Friday Mine in
Idaho's rich Coeur d'Alene mining district near
Wallace. The shaft, which will greatly increase
the production capacity of the silver mine, descends 6200 feet, and may eventually be deepened
to 7500 feet. The region around Wallace, histori-
cally rich in silver and lead, has some of the
world's largest and deepest silver mines; some
100-year-old mines contain 200 miles of tunnels.

THE LAST

1. MOSQUITO FLEET SHIP: The VIRGINIA V is the
last of Seattle's famed Mosquito Fleet, and the
last inland-water, passenger-carrying steamer east
of the Mississippi, one of two in the U.S.
    Built in 1922, she was one of 500 steamers
that carried passengers, freight and mail to small
communities isolated on the shores of Puget Sound
for 70 years. That Mosquito Fleet was the largest
of its kind in the world.
    For 17 years the VIRGINIA V steamed daily be-
tween Tacoma and Seattle, covering 320,000 miles
and carrying 8 million people. At that time the
Mosquito Fleet was almost the only way to move
from one settlement to another. Roads were
scarce, land travel difficult, private boats few.
    But cars, roads and bridges became common in
the late 1920s and 1930s; so did private ferries,
and then, a state ferry system. Most of the Mosquito Fleet boats were salvaged for scrap metal
and then burned.
    But VIRGINIA V was unusually sturdy, built of
heavy timbers. So, despite a 1934 windstorm that
blew off her pilothouse and collapsed her upper

decks, she continued to steam on the Sound: excursions; carrying World War II soldiers on weekend leave from Fort Worden; a run on the Columbia between Portland and Astoria; the Tacoma-Seattle run for 3 years; excursions again.

But she was showing her age, expensive to run, her timbers rotting. Saved by a group of volunteers, she was entered on the National Register of Historic Places in 1973, and the Virginia V Foundation was formed in 1976. With grants and volunteer labor, the old ship was refurbished, superstructure rebuilt, engine overhauled, cabin decks and pilothouse rebuilt.

Today, rented to private groups, she cruises the Sound-- Port Townsend, Gig Harbor, Poulsbo-- sounding her full-throated brass steam whistle.

2. LIGHTSHIP: The last lightship on active duty on the West Coast, the COLUMBIA, is now moored in Astoria Maritime Park near Columbia River Maritime Museum, one of the best such museums in the West. The ship, retired in 1961, served off the mouth of the Columbia for two decades.

THE MOST

1. MOST OFTEN CLIMBED: Mount Hood, 11,235' high, is North America's most frequently climbed glaciated peak and Oregon's highest mountain. With 12 glaciers and 5 ridges, it offers both advanced and relatively easy routes. Discovered and named in

1792, Mount Hood is Oregon's only volcano from which eruptions were observed by pioneers.

Mount Hood has the largest fumarole fields of any Oregon volcano, heavily scented by hydrogen sulphide gas. The intense heat and moisture alters summit rocks, causing mudflows and avalanches. Once, the mountain was 1000' higher, before mudflows and heavy glaciation lowered it. During the Ice Age, an ice cap nearly covered it.

In 1956 the largest rescue operation ever to occur in the Cascades took place on Mount Hood, after a descending climber slipped while tied on a 240-foot-long rope to 17 others. One person died; 13 had to be carried down on litters.

MOUNT HOOD: North America's most frequently climbed glaciated peak (Oregon Dept. of Geology & Mineral Industries)

2. STEAMERS: At one time Lake Coeur d'Alene, one of the Northwest's most beautiful lakes, floated the most steam vessels of any lake west of the Mississippi. The first steamer, built in 1880 was used by the U.S. Army to carry supplies. Two others, built on Lake Coeur d'Alene were used from 1883-84 to haul passengers and freight. Eventually there were fleets of steamers. After gold was exhausted, silver, zinc and lead were mined.

The many Idaho Panhandle rivers and lakes, Ice Age and Spokane Flood heritage, were highways for prospectors, miners, loggers and settlers following the trappers and missionaries. Small steamers towed log rafts, and carried ore from mines to mills, and crops and cattle from remote farms and ranches to railheads and markets. Sailing up the Coeur d'Alene River, they carried supplies for miners working in canyons to the east.

3. RHODES SCHOLARS: Oregon's Reed College has produced the most Rhodes scholars of any liberal arts college in the U.S.-- 29. It ranks first among the nation's undergraduate institutions in the number of graduates who get their Ph.D.-- 1 of every 5.2. The 1128 students are North America's only undergraduates to have their own on-campus nuclear reactor.

4. CEMETERIES: Roslyn, Washington has the most cemeteries of any U.S. city of its size-- 24, with 2500 graves. This historic coal boomtown, active from 1886 to the 1920s, peaked at 5000 people, mostly immigrants: Italians, Serbians, Slavs, Poles, Welsh, Scots, English. Each group had its own taverns, churches, social lodges, and cemetery. Since all cemeteries were on the same hill, they have gradually merged. The Brick Tavern, oldest licensed tavern in Washington, has a spittoon trough with running water.

5. WESTERNMOST CITY: Port Orford, Oregon, is the westernmost incorporated city in the lower 48. Located just south of Cape Blanco, westernmost headland, it has Oregon's westernmost lighthouse.

6. POWER BOATS: The Puget Sound area has the most pleasure boats owned per capita in the U.S. and probably in the world-- 250,000. Washington has the most saltwater marine parks in the nation, 35, more than all other states combined. Hiram M. Chittenden Locks in Seattle-- the locks that connect saltwater Puget Sound with the higher, freshwater Lakes Union and Washington-- are one of the busiest locks in the U.S., primarily because of so many pleasure boats (80,000 vessels a year). Finished in 1917, they are the oldest locks operating in the Pacific Northwest.

Before the construction of the locks and the 8-mile-long Lake Washington Ship Canal, there was no direct route between these points. The lack of a waterway between Lakes Washington and Union inspired the Northwest's most unlikely one-man digging project. In 1860 Harvey Pike began to dig by shovel a shallow canal between the two lakes. In 1880 a canal association hired 25 laborers to dig it deep enough to float logs and small ships.

Migrating salmon also use the locks to return to spawning grounds in the Lake Washington system.

7. BASQUES: Idaho has the most Basques of any place outside the Pyrenees, 20,000. Originally, many came from the French and Spanish Pyrenees in 1890-92, attracted by California's gold fields. Many later headed for Idaho, whose mountains reminded them of their home. Although they began as sheepherders and ranch hands, most Basques now work in many different fields.

The Basques maintain their culture, the unique and difficult language, and traditions such as the pelota, a handball-like game, and the jota, a dance noted for its fast footwork.

The sheepherder tradition continues strong, with Sheepherder Balls held in January in a number of Idaho valley towns. In late July Basques from Boise's thriving Basque Center celebrate with a weekend picnic, music, dancing and a Mass.

BASQUE SHEEPHERDER: Idaho has the most Basques outside the Pyrenees (Idaho Travel Council)

8. SEAPORT: Lewiston, Idaho, became the West's most inland seaport in 1975 after the completion of a series of dams on the Lower Snake River permitted shallow-draft navigation. Ocean-going tugs and barges now travel through the locks of 8 dams 464 miles up the Columbia and Snake Rivers to the city, Idaho's lowest spot, 738' above sea level. Lewiston was an early trade center for merchants, miners, trappers, and homesteaders after gold was discovered in 1860 in nearby mountains. It was Idaho's territorial capital in 1863.

9. SOVEREIGNTY: England granted to Hudson's Bay Company in 1670 the most sweeping sovereignty ever given a commercial company. The company received absolute proprietorship over a region of unknown extent in North America, 10 times the size of the Holy Roman Empire. Their jurisdiction in civil and military affairs was unquestioned; they could make laws, even declare war against the "pagans."

HBC is the world's oldest surviving English-language business corporation and the world's second-best documented institution (next to the Vatican). Parliament merged the North West Company and HBC in 1821 because intense rivalry between the two created financial problems for both.

In 1824 the new HBC governor George Simpson arrived in the Northwest to reorganize the company. With him was Dr. John McLoughlin, who was Chief Factor of Fort Vancouver for 20 years. He provided virtually the region's only government until the treaty in 1846 settled the boundary dispute between the U.S. and Canada.

10. SCUBA DIVERS: The most scuba divers in the Northwest, third largest number in the U.S., live in Washington: 250,000. Despite the frigid water of Puget Sound and the Strait of Juan de Fuca, where most of them dive, the sport is popular, because of water clarity (especially in winter), and the diversity, color and size of animal species. Modern dry suits make the cold water tolerable.

The only city-owned underwater park on the U.S. Pacific Coast is at Edmonds, Washington. Created in 1970, the park protects one of the Northwest's most popular, most accessible and interesting scuba-diving locations. 5,000 divers a year from many states explore an underwater area in which sea life is attracted to an assortment of objects: a 300'-long drydock, originally sunk as a ferry dock breakwater; 2 tugs; a 30'-long sailboat and other wooden boats; concrete rubble, old tires

SCUBA DIVING: Edmonds, Washington has the West Coast's only city-owned scuba-diving park (Saling)

and a "jungle gym" of steel shelving. Making the Edmonds park superb for diving are a stable accreting beach, minor currents, and shallow water.

Puget Sound has some of the nation's most interesting, scenic waters for scuba diving. Glacial ice scouring out the trough of Puget Sound left huge boulders, spectacular submarine reefs and cliffs plunging hundreds of feet in the Strait of Juan de Fuca and San Juan Islands. In places, animal life is so rich that divers can scarcely touch bottom without disturbing some organism.

11. VOLCANOES: Portland has the most volcanoes in or near its city limits of any U.S. city. It may be the only major U.S. city to have within its limits cinder cones that are not extinct. Within 13 miles are at least 32 centers of past volcanic activity. Most are well-known buttes: Rocky Butte, Powell Butte, Mount Tabor (which forms a natural amphitheatre used in summer for musical events).

12. COVERED BRIDGES: The Northwest has the most covered bridges of any area in the U.S., nearly 60. The first was built in 1851 in Oregon City. Oregon has the most; early Willamette Valley settlers, who came from New England, duplicated the bridges common there. Grays River Bridge in Washington is the Northwest's oldest, built in 1905, the only one of four there that is for public use.

Oregon has 52 covered bridges remaining out of 450 built, all but one west of the Cascades. Many are still used; others have been bypassed by modern bridges. Floods, fires, and rotting destroyed many. The oldest in Oregon is Mosby Creek Bridge (1920); Portland has the newest (1981).

Styles differ, but all had to have rounded portals high and wide enough for a wagonload of hay to pass through. Walls could be solid with slit windows near the roof, or with eye level, "day-lighting" windows, or exposed wall trusses for light and a view of oncoming traffic.

Most are in the Willamette Valley, from Albany to Cottage Grove. For early bridges, big trees close to the creek or river were felled across it, then shaped on site with adzes and broad axes. Douglas fir was preferred, for strength, length, and lightness.

Settlers cooperated to build the earliest ones but soon there were toll bridges. A horseman paid 10 to 50 cents; a wagon, up to $2. Arguments over tolls were common. By 1857, the bridges were free, built by the government.

Almost all are one-lane. In the early days when two wagons met head-on, fights might erupt over who had the "courtesy of the bridge."

Bridges were covered in the rainy Northwest to prevent trusses from getting wet and rotting, and to strengthen the bridge. Uncovered, a bridge lasts only 10 to 20 years; covered, more than 100.

Uses were varied: shelter from rain, lynching, fishing platform, courting, weddings, funerals. The first Shimanek bridge even had a two-holer.

13. VICTORIAN TOWN: Port Townsend, Washington, a National Historic District, is the most authentic Victorian seacoast town, with the best preserved buildings of any city north of San Francisco.

Founded in 1851 at the strategically located entrance to Puget Sound, Port Townsend was a U.S. Port of Entry in the late 19th century. In 1889 her natural harbor was second in the U.S. to New York City's in volume of ship traffic.

City leaders expected the town to become Puget Sound's commercial center, but it never recovered from the Crash of 1893, or its failure to get a railroad terminus, as Tacoma did.

During the boom years, huge homes were built on the bluff overlooking the water, away from the rowdy waterfront. They are noted for stained glass windows, handmade stair banisters, widow's walks, muraled ceilings, gabled cupolas, French Mansard roofs. More than 40 city buildings are Registered Historical Places, including Jefferson County Courthouse (1892), one of the two oldest in Washington. The oldest house is Capt. Enoch Fowler's, (c. 1860). The largest, with 27 rooms, is Manresa Castle (1892), built by the first mayor.

STARRETT HOUSE (1889)

14. MOST VARIED BUILDINGS: Albany has the North-west's most architecturally varied collection of historic buildings, dating from the 1840's through the 1920s. Its three National Historic Districts encompass 100 square blocks.

The lavish homes in Monteith District, with 88 notable structures built in 9 major architectural styles, reflect Albany's prosperity as Willamette Valley's manufacturing and transportation center. A steamboat first called at Albany in 1852; by 1866, five riverboats were making regular runs between Albany, Corvallis and Portland.

Monteith House, Albany's first frame house (1849), was built by the two Monteith brothers who founded the city. Hackleman District includes 55 buildings in 12 styles, including Ralston House (1889) in elaborate Queen Anne style.

The original city center has survived, with 42 old commercial buildings in the Downtown District. Among them is one of several "fire-proof" brick buildings (1866); the only original wood frame commercial building left (c. 1875); and the oldest waterfront building, Avery Mill (1866).

THE HIGHEST

1. LOCKS: The locks of John Day Dam, built in 1863, are the highest single-lift locks on the Columbia, and the world's deepest. Equipped with a gate weighing 1100 tons, they can raise ships 113' in 15 minutes between Lakes Umatilla and Celillo. The downgate is unusual in opening vertically.

2. DAM: Swift Dam, built in 1958 over the North Fork of Washington's Lewis River, is the highest earthfill dam in the Northwest, 2nd highest in the U.S., 610' high by 2100' long.

3. DAM: Washington's Grand Coulee Dam over the Columbia River is the Northwest's 2nd highest, the nation's 3rd highest, at 550'. Its height was limited so that it would not flood into Canada.

4. DAM: Idaho's Dworshak Dam, a gravity dam built in 1974 on the North Fork of the Clearwater River, is the Northwest's highest dam, 3rd highest dam in the U.S. at 717', and the largest straight-axis dam in North America, 3287' long.

DWORSHAK DAM: highest Northwest dam, North America's largest straight-axis dam (Idaho Travel Council)

5. BUILDING: The highest building west of Chicago and north of Houston was topped off in Seattle in 1984. The 76-story Columbia Seafirst Center,

943 feet high, is primarily an office building, holding 6000 people. The view it provides for the public is much inferior to the view from the top, reserved for a private club. A 1985 poll showed that 71-year-old Smith Tower, once the tallest building west of the Mississippi at 522', was still Seattle's favorite.

THE LONGEST

1. HIKING TRAIL: The nation's longest hiking trail is the Pacific Crest Trail, which runs for 2400 miles from Washington's northern border down through California. In the Northwest it follows the Cascades, dipping into canyons and the desert. One of its most challenging parts crosses Rainy Pass (4843') and Washington Pass (5483). Covering 453 miles of Washington and 420 miles of Oregon, it runs mainly through national forest and park land. It was established in 1968 by the National Scenic Trails System Act, along with the 2000-mile Appalachian Trail.

2. FLOATING BRIDGE: Washington's Evergreen Point bridge is the world's longest pontoon bridge of reenforced concrete, 12,596' long. Its floating section is 7518'-- 1.42 miles long. Finished in 1963, it spans Lake Washington, as does Lacey V. Murrow Bridge, the world's first floating bridge and second longest at 6561'. It was built in 1940 to join Mercer Island to Seattle. The two are among the world's largest pontoon bridges.

The world's third longest floating bridge-- the world's longest over tidewater-- is the Hood Canal Floating Bridge, 6471' long. It joins Kitsap and Olympic Peninsulas south of Hood Canal's entrance. Larger and heavier than the Evergreen Bridge, it is the largest floating structure ever

built anywhere, stretching over tidal water with
heavy currents and surface waves. Water levels
can vary up to 18 vertical feet a day.

The present bridge, finished in late 1982, re-
places a bridge built in 1961 that was broken up
by an unusually intense storm in February 1981,
with sustained winds reaching 80 mph, gusting at
100 mph. Anchors and pontoons on the new bridge,
which includes part of the old one, are heavier.

Required to be large enough to handle Bangor
Submarine Base nuclear submarines, which need a
600-foot navigable channel, it has the world's
longest drawspan.

3. RAILROAD TUNNEL: The Cascade Tunnel of Burlington Northern Railroad, built through the Cascades at Stevens Pass in 1929, is the Western
Hemisphere's longest railroad tunnel, 7.8 miles--
1388 yards. It drops to 2nd place in October,
1986 when a longer Canadian tunnel opens. Next
longest is the Burlington Northern Flathead Tunnel, 1319 yards.

4. FERRY RUN: The nation's longest regular state
ferry run, and one of the world's most scenic,
winds through the San Juan Islands. The Washington State ferry run begins at Anacortes and ends
at Sidney, Vancouver Island, B.C. The 36.7-mile-
long-trip takes 2 1/4 hours without stops-- the
usual summer run-- and 4 hours with stops at several San Juan Islands. Two trips a day are made
in summer; one a day, the rest of the year.

5. BRIDGE: Portland's Fremont Bridge is North
America's 3rd longest steel arch bridge at 1255
feet. Another unnamed Portland bridge over the
Willamette River, built in 1908, is North America's longest swing span bridge at 521 feet.

6. BRIDGE: North America's longest continuous truss bridge, Megler Bridge (4.1 miles), crosses the Columbia River from Long Beach Peninsula to Astoria, replacing a ferry in 1966. Supporting towers 1200' apart leave a channel of 1070', large enough for the U.S. Navy's biggest battleship.

Long ago, people sometimes crossed the Columbia at this spot by <u>kedging.</u> That involved being on a raft and repeatedly heaving an anchor out as far as possible, pulling the raft to it, hauling up the anchor and throwing it out again.

THE ONLY

1. GLASS SCHOOL: The world's only school devoted solely to glass art is Washington's Pilchuck Glass School. The focus is on glass as an art form. Founded in 1971 by glass artist Dale Chihuly with the help of Seattle art patrons John Hauberg and Anne Gould Hauberg, the school has made the Seattle area internationally known for the artistic works of its innovative glass artists.

Open only during the summer, it attracts both talented beginners and glass artists of international stature. Classes, taught by visiting instructors and artists-in-residence, are two and three weeks long, and stress creative technique in working with hot glass, carving, design. Furnaces in the open-sided hot-glass building are used 24 hours a day as teams of four artists work eight-hour shifts.

The school, located on 40 wooded acres in the Skagit Valley at 1000' elevation, is noted for its rustic wooden buildings and creative isolation.

2. TELESCOPE: The only telescope in the world as large as 24 1/2" (600X magnification) available to the public is located at Goldendale Observatory in eastern Washington, a state park since 1980. 10% of the time is reserved for personal projects of amateur astronomers, after 11 p.m.

Because of clear skies and the lack of light pollution, the mountaintop site was chosen in 1979 as Official Eclipse Observing Station for the last total solar eclipse visible in the U.S. in the 20th century. For the first solar eclipse of the century in 1918, professional astronomers brought portable equipment to the site.

Eastern Oregon's Pine Mountain is the Northwest's only full-time research observatory. Oldest Northwest observatory is at Linfield College, Oregon, with an 1890s telescope. Manatash Observatory near Ellensburg has the second largest telescope west of the Mississippi (30") for educational use-- U.W. graduate student research.

3. OPERA: The Seattle Opera is the only opera company in the Western Hemisphere to perform each year since 1975, within a week, the four operas of Wagner's complete Ring Cycle. Scheduled for August 1986 was a controversial modernized version, with two complete cycles in German, and supratitles in English.

4. LIFEBOAT SCHOOL: The Coast Guard National Motor Lifeboat School is the world's only professional school for training Coast Guard and other selected students to handle motorboats in rough surf. It was founded in 1968 near the Columbia River mouth at Cape Disappointment Station, home of Washington's largest search-and-rescue facilities for vessels in trouble.

Classrooms are at the Cape; boats are launched at nearby Ilwaco. Coast Guard personnel learn launching and surf-and-rescue techniques in 44' and 52' self-righting motorboats that can survive 30' waves in "the nastiest water in the U.S."

5. BRIDGE: The Tacoma Narrows Bridge is the only bridge that crosses Puget Sound. It has the 5th longest center span of any North American suspension bridge, 2800'; its total length is 5979'.

The four-lane bridge was completed in 1952, 12 years after its predecessor, nicknamed "Galloping Gertie," broke up in a high wind and fell into the Sound. Gertie departed this world at age 4 months and 7 days. But only the main span was lost. Reused in the new bridge were undamaged piers and anchorages, and the western approach, only slightly damaged. Major changes, with improved aerodynamics, were made in the new center span.

TACOMA NARROWS BRIDGE: only bridge crossing Puget Sound
(Bob & Ira Spring)

6. GOLF: Soda Springs, Idaho, has the world's only golf course with a 135-year-old historical hazard: foot-deep Oregon Trail wagon wheel ruts.

7. WAR ATTACK: The only mainland U.S. military installation to be fired on during World War II and the first attack in 130 years, since the War of 1812, by an enemy firing at a continental U.S. fortification was Fort Stevens, Oregon. It was built in Civil War days 10 miles south of Astoria to guard the mouth of the Columbia River against Confederate gunboats. In June 1942 a Japanese submarine about 10 miles out at sea fired nine shells close to the fort, but no damage resulted.

The fort's Battery Russell was famous for cannons that could disappear after each firing, but, knowing that the guns lacked the range, Americans did not return the Japanese fire.

8. CHIMPANZEE SPEECH: The nation's only primate center where chimpanzees are taught American Sign Language is found at Central Washington University in Ellensburg. This is the nation's only strictly behavioral (not medical) chimpanzee research program. Running the program is one of the world's leading researchers in the study of language acquisition by chimpanzees, psychology professor Roger Fouts. His wife Debbi helps him.

Fout has worked for 17 years with the star of the CWU program, 20-year-old Washoe, raised since birth like a human child. The first chimp to use a human language, the language of the deaf, she has a vocabulary of some 176 signs, and combines signs to create meanings for unfamiliar situations and objects. Anyone who knows sign language can converse with her. She uses nouns, pronouns, adjectives, proper names, verbs, and prepositions, and can string them together into sentences. She has taught signs to four other chimps at the center, and to human volunteers.

Part of the money used to fund the program, which receives no government grants, came from pay Fouts received as technical adviser to the movie, "Greystoke: The Legend of Tarzan."

9.   LAND: Point Roberts, Washington is the only land in the lower 48 that can be reached only by sea or by traveling across foreign land (Canada). It became American after the 1872 arbitration of San Juan Island boundaries by Kaiser Wilhelm I.

10. STATE NAME: Washington is the only state to bear a U.S. president's name. "Columbia" was the first choice, but Washington D.C. residents feared confusion. The result: "The Other Washington."

11. PLANETARIUM: The only planetarium in Washington owned by a college is Willard Geer Planetarium of Bellevue Community College. Inspired by a distinguished scientist on the faculty who held patents on color TV, the planetarium, built in 1974, is the most active teaching planetarium in the state for schools and the public.

It was western Washington's first major planetarium and the first public-supported one. It is also the largest with a 30' aluminum dome and seats for 65. It owns the most special effects projectors of any Washington planetarium.

The "star ball" end of its Spitz 4A projector reproduces 1352 stars with the most accuracy of any state planetarium. Its opposite end projects the sun, the moon and the five visible planets.

Seattle's Skylab Planetarium at Pacific Science Center has one of Washington's largest portable telescopes (16") and the Northwest's only portable inflatable planetariums, for school use.

12. AQUARIUM: The Seattle Aquarium is the only public aquarium in the world to have a fish ladder and salmon culture program that generates its own salmon run. It has one of only two salt-water fishladders in the world. Salmon were released at the aquarium site in 1975, two years before the new waterfront aquarium and its fish ladder were

completed. The first salmon returned in 1978, en-
tering the ladder from Elliott Bay, and swimming
against the current through two dozen levels until
they reach fresh water. In the spawning season
they can be viewed through two overhead viewing
windows, one as they pass the middle of the ladder
and the other at the top step where they are held
until they ripen. There the females are stripped
of eggs, and milt is squeezed over them. In 1984,
117 salmon returned, both coho and chum.

The aquarium has the world's most successful
sea otter breeding program. A pup born in 1979,
the only aquarium-born pup ever to survive for any
length of time, is still alive. Of five others
born, three were alive at the end of 1985. In
August 1983 two northern fur seal pups were born
at the aquarium, the first ever born to mothers
raised in captivity.

The Seattle Aquarium had the world's first and
only giant Pacific octopus (Octopus dofleini,
found only in Puget Sound) which went through its
entire life cycle from egg to death as an adult in
captivity. O'Toole, born in 1982, was the sole
survivor of 200 larvae. He lived 3 years and 2
months, reaching a normal 65 pounds with tentacle
length of 5 feet. He died of old age at the end
of 1985, after refusing to eat and wasting away.

13. LOCOMOTIVE: The only geared locomotive produced in the U.S. was the Willamette locomotive.
The engines were made especially for the Northwest's steep grades and sharp curves. Some of the
old locomotives can be seen in Oregon town parks.

THE MOST OUTSTANDING

1. SHAKESPEAREAN FESTIVAL: Oregon's southernmost
city, Ashland, presents the most outstanding and

oldest annual Shakepearean Festival in the Western
Hemisphere. The town of 15,000 people, located in
a Siskiyou foothill rainshadow, was an early stage
coach stop, the only town on the western Oregon
Chatauqua circuit to build a permanent structure
for the lecture series.

Angus Bowman, a drama and English teacher in
Ashland, put on the first festival in 1935. Three
performances of 2 Shakespeare plays were given in
a make-shift outdoor theatre. The budget: $400.

The 1985 budget was $5.1 million; audience,
350,000; number of performances, 643; plays, 11.
The eight-month season begins with an indoor
season in late February. The resident company
is among the nation's six best.

Shakespeare's plays are always presented in
the outdoor Globe Theatre, the oldest authentic
reproduction of Shakespeare's Fortune theatre in
London in the Western Hemisphere. A rare 1632
folio is among the 5000-volume Shakespeare collection at Southern Oregon State College library.

ASHLAND SHAKESPEAREAN FESTIVAL: *Western Hemisphere's oldest*
Shakespearean festival, in Oregon's southernmost city
(Ashland Chamber of Commerce - Hank Kranzler)

2. MEDICAL FACILITIES: The Northwest has some of the nation's most outstanding medical facilities. These are unusually concentrated, because the excellent medical schools draw many specialists, and also because the region has far fewer economically and socially disadvantaged people than many large eastern U.S. cities. Thus, researchers here can work on sophisticated medical procedures.

The U.W. Medical School made the first practical long-term use in the U.S. of the kidney dialysis machine. Their decentralized Family Medicine training program for medical students is a model for others in the U.S. For the past decade the U.W. Medical School has been among the top three of the nation in Bio-Medical research. It is foremost in the nation in research on Alzheimer's disease, with two nationally funded centers.

The University of Oregon Medical School and Portland medical facilities are internationally recognized for the development of artificial heart valves and heart valve treatment. Located at the Portland facilities is the Oregon Elks Children's Eye Clinic, one of the major such clinics in the world. Idaho is at the forefront of clinical cancer treatment. Seattle's Fred Hutchinson Cancer Research Center, housed at Swedish Hospital, leads the world in bone marrow transplants.

Seattle's Harborview Hospital has an outstanding Burn Treatment Center. Providence Hospital, Seattle's oldest, is outstanding in cardiovascular surgery, second in the West for number of open-heart surgery operations, yet a leader in alternatives to bypass, such as repairing blocked coronary arteries. It has one of the nation's few Sleep-Wake Centers for diagnosis and treatment of sleep disorders. Swedish Hospital is the Northwest's largest health care complex, housing three specialized major health care centers.

Washington's Group Health Cooperative is the nation's largest consumer-governed health maintenance organization (HMO) with 315,000 members in

1985, 4th largest HMO in the nation. Begun in 1947 it was one of the nation's first cooperative pre-paid medical groups, a prototype for others.

The Seattle Fire Department's Medic I program of emergency response care was one of the nation's first three, started simultaneously in 1970. Seattle Medic I vans have one of the fastest response times in the U.S. for cardiac emergencies-- 3 minutes. Medic II teams teach cardiopulmonary resuscitation (CPR) to the public; in King County 40% of the population over 12 has learned CPR, by far, the nation's highest rate.

The Lions Eye Bank, located at the University of Washington hospital since 1969, is the largest in the U.S. that takes only donated eyes. It is unusual in its interaction with donor families, and in being solely supported by the Lions Club. In addition to transplants, donated eyes provide tissue, nerves, sclera and retinas.

The regional PNW Poison Center Network, begun in 1956 for children and expanded for adults, is one of the best such programs in the U.S. It operates a 24-hour hot line for instant first-aid information and referrals to treatment facilities. Based at Seattle's Children's Orthopedic Hospital, the center covers Idaho, Alaska and Washington.

3. ZOO: Seattle's Woodland Park Zoo is outstanding in the U.S. for breeding rare animals and for innovative, naturalistic design of animal areas, for which it won a #1 rating from the National Division of the Humane Society. Parade Magazine in 1984 named it one of the 10 best zoos in the U.S. Its docent training program is the most comprehensive in the world.

Woodland Park Zoo has one of the world's best nocturnal houses, and an outstanding African Savanna. Its half-acre tropical forest gorilla habitat is among the largest of any U.S. zoo.

The zoo has a long list of firsts in breeding

animals, with many rare births and hatchings: red pandas, Humboldt penguins, golden lion tamarins, endangered snow leopards, Malayan sun bears; a baby tree hyrax in 1983, the first ever, outside its native habitat; the hatching of two Hartlaubs ducks in 1977, a Western Hemisphere first; three common trumpeter chicks (native to the Amazon), the world's first captive-born, in 1984; first gila monster young in the West; first Brazilian tapir (1983); and in early 1986, four yellow-spotted, side-necked turtles (after 18 years of failure). Only one other zoo in the nation has ever hatched any of the rare turtles.

Woodland Park Zoo began as a menagerie on the 196-acre Green Lake estate of Guy Phinney. When Seattle bought it in 1899 for $100,000, residents complained it was too distant and too costly.

WOODLAND PARK ZOO: Brazilian tapir is one of zoo's many firsts in rare animal breeding (Woodland Park Zoo- Hank Klein)

4. EXPLORATION: The most outstandingly important, difficult and successful journey of land exploration ever made to the Northwest, and one of
the most significant in American history, was undertaken in 1804-06 by Meriwether Lewis and William Clark, the most competent explorers in the
nation's history.

President Jefferson approved $2500 for the
trip-- perhaps the biggest bargain in the history
of travel. The President's goal was "to find the
shortest and most convenient route of communica-
tion between the U.S. and the Pacific Ocean." But
more important, the expedition laid the basis for
later claims by the U.S. to the Pacific Northwest.
The "Corps of Discovery" was important, also, in
encouraging Americans to go west.

The two young men-- in 1805 Clark was 35 and
Lewis, 31-- shared command with no serious dispute
in spite of mountains much higher and rivers much
more treacherous than expected. The expedition
traveled 8000 miles round-trip from St. Louis. In
2 years of wilderness travel, only one man died.

President Jefferson asked each to keep a journal, describing Indian customs, geography, plants,
animals, commercial opportunities, climate, minerals. The Lewis and Clark journals are among the
most interesting any American explorers wrote.

The expedition prepared the way for the Astorians 5 years later in 1811 to establish an American fur-trading post near Astoria. They were barely two months ahead of David Thompson of the North
West Company, who traveled down the Columbia, hop-
ing to establish a British fort on the Pacific.

One of the Northwest's most scenic, historic
and difficult-to-build highways, Idaho's Lewis and
Clark Highway (U.S. #12), roughly parallels or
touches the expedition's path over 5233-foot-high
Lolo Pass, across the Bitterroots, down into the
Snake River Valley. Unable to canoe on the dan-
gerous Salmon River, the expedition traveled over
Lolo Pass, one of the most difficult sections of

the journey. Clark wrote that he would never forget how they suffered during the nine days spent on the steep Indian trail, so clogged with rocks and fallen trees it was almost impassable. There was little grass for the horses, and little fresh meat for the men. On the return trip, the tired men bathed in steaming Lolo Pass hot springs.

5. STATE PARKS: Oregon has one of the most outstanding state park systems in the U.S. with more than 233 parks, waysides and recreation areas. Its 83,380-acre park system is one of the West's most extensive. Nearly 50 parks, recreation areas or waysides dot the scenic Oregon Coast route.

The smorgasbord of parks includes a pioneer homestead, an old Indian burial ground, a bog of carnivorous pitcher plants, driftwood beaches, a stagecoach route with two stagecoach stations, lava caves, Crown Point in the Columbia Gorge, an authentic military fort, Crane Prairie Reservoir with its many ospreys, a myrtle grove, Silver Falls State Park, and much more.

6. HISTORIC PERSON: Oregon's most outstanding historic personage was Dr. John McLoughlin, Chief Factor for 20 years of the Hudson's Bay Company Fort Vancouver. Thousands of Oregon Trail emigrants benefitted from his intelligent management of the fort and its many agricultural and commercial activities. This "Father of Oregon," also called the "Despot of the Rockies," strongly influenced the settlement of the Northwest, providing order where there was no government.

Although Britain and America had a joint occupation agreement for Oregon Country, McLoughlin discouraged emigrants from settling north of the Columbia, a region Britain was determined to keep. He provided valuable services to the emigrants he diverted south to the Willamette Valley. His HBC

stores extended credit to hundreds of them in 1843
and 1844, selling them clothing, shoes, hardware,
tools, seeds, coffee, salt and sugar. Many never
paid off their HBC debts.

McLoughlin made Fort Vancouver the most outstanding of all Northwest trading-post forts, and
the Northwest's most important settlement, half-
way between San Francisco and Russian Alaskan. It
is really the birthplace of the Pacific Northwest.

The move from Fort George (formerly Fort Astoria) to a location north of the Columbia was
made partly to establish Britain's claim to that
territory, and partly so that food could be raised
to supply other western HBC fur-trading forts.

The new fort, first built on a bluff above the
Columbia in 1825, was rebuilt in 1829, closer to
the river, near the eastern limits of today's Vancouver. Inside the 20'-high stockade were some 40
buildings-- warehouses, workshops, offices, and,
in the center, McLoughlin's 2-story house. In its

FORT VANCOUVER: *most outstanding Northwest trading-post fort in
1845 (Oregon Historical Society- J.H. Warre sketch)*

common dining room, kilted pipers entertained as guests ate from English china and were served from sterling silver dishes.

After the boundaries of Oregon Country were settled in 1846, Fort Vancouver, now on American soil, was taken over by the Americans. McLoughlin retired to Oregon City. Closed in 1860, the fort was destroyed by fire in 1866.

Near the fort, the first U.S. Army post in the Northwest was built in 1849. The oldest house remaining, built of sheathed logs in Southern Plantation style, is Grant House (1849), in which General Grant lived as quartermaster (1852-1853). The city of Vancouver, oldest continuous settlement in Washington, owns many of the 19 pre-Civil-War houses that still stand in Officers Row, one of only three such groups remaining in the U.S.

7. CITY PARK: Tacoma's Point Defiance Park is one of the Northwest's most outstanding and most varied urban parks, combining public attractions with wild areas. Once a military reservation, the site, eight miles northwest of downtown Tacoma and surrounded on three sides by Puget Sound, was given to the city in 1888. Much of it remains undeveloped except for hiking trails.

It includes an extensively remodeled zoo and aquarium; a 20-acre, outdoor logging museum, Camp Six, with equipment and artifacts from the era of steam logging; a 5-mile bicycle trail; dahlia and rose gardens; a Japanese garden; one of the West Coast's biggest and most colorful displays of annual flowers-- 30,000; a driftwood beach; reconstructed Fort Nisqually with Washington's oldest building (the granary-- 1843); and the boiler of the Beaver, the Northwest's first steamship.

A unique Northwest Native Garden displays native plants in different Northwest climatic and geographic zones. The zoo and aquarium feature naturalistic habitats and Pacific Rim wildlife.

An award-winning polar bear exhibit allows viewing
the bears through split-level windows, above and
below the water. The zoo has the world's largest
captive population of rare red wolves, which it
breeds.

8. ARCHEOLOGY: The most outstanding archeological site discovered in the Northwest was Marmes
Rock Shelter in southeastern Washington's Palouse
Canyon. Human bones found there are some of the
oldest human remains in the Western Hemisphere to
be so well documented and protected.

The site gives clues to plant and animal life,
and the climate of thousands of years ago. Never
before has such a long sequence of events been so
well documented at one site. Washington State
University archeologists took back to their laboratory samples of eight layers, covering 20,000
years, the world's only such laboratory record.

Layers up to 12,000 years old produced hunting
points, oldest known in the Western Hemisphere,
similar to those found among mammoth bones. In one
cave 15 Indian skeletons, dating from 8000 years
ago, were found buried-- North America's oldest
known ancient burial. Under Mazama ash, burned
skeletons 9000 years old were found, perhaps the
oldest cremation site in the world.

With the bones were found 250 artifacts, many
finely worked: mortars and pestles, hide scrapers,
hammer stones of opal, obsidian and jasper. Rare
bone needles were found, some with eyes.

Research ended when the Lower Monumental Dam
on Snake River flooded the site. A levee had been
built to protect the site, but it failed.

9. SKI RESORT: Idaho's Sun Valley is the most
outstanding ski resort in the Northwest, and North
America's best all-round ski area, according to a
1985 survey by Ski Magazine.   The first U.S. ski

resort, Sun Valley was built in 1936 by Union Pacific Railroad to increase passenger travel.

Famous for powder snow, it has 16 lifts and 66 ski runs; the best is 9151' Baldy Mountain. Its original chair lift, the world's first, was patterned after a ship-dock banana conveyor belt.

10. HISTORICAL SOCIETY: Oregon Historical Society is one of the nation's most outstanding, with North America's largest per capita enrollment for a historical society-- more than 8000 members. Incorporated in 1898, OHS was formed from the Oregon Pioneer Association (1873).

Its Regional Research Library, with 17 million manuscripts, photographs, maps, books, microfilms, and scholarly journals unavailable elsewhere, is the world's most complete Northwest library.

The six-floor OHS building in Portland's Washington Park has been called the finest modern historical building in America.

11. MASTODON KILL SITE: An outstanding archeological find in 1977 near Sequim, on the Olympic Peninsula, was Manis Mastodon Site, only mastodon kill site ever found in North America. Imbedded in a mastodon rib found in a boggy area was a bone spear point of different bone, dated about 12,000 years. Bones revealed arthritis and partial healing of the wound; thus, the animal lived for a few months after being wounded. A stone chopping or cutting tool nearby was used for the butchering.

Two years later in Michigan, mastodon bones, burned and scraped, were found, but no weapon.

The Manis find proved that human and mastodon co-existed in the Northwest. A nearby camp showed use by 12 separate cultures covering 5200 years. A firepit with charred fragments of bison bones resting on glacial deposits indicates the kill was made after the Ice Age, 14,000 years ago.

12. LODGE: Mount Hood's Timberline Lodge is outstanding in the nation for its hand-crafted, hand-
hewn character. Built as a W.P.A. project in the
'30s, it cannot be matched by any other large,
still-used public building in the nation for quality or amount of handwork. Both animal and plant
motifs are featured throughout. There are wrought
iron lamps, gate, hinges, straps; stained glass
Paul Bunyan murals; wood-relief carvings; hand-
hewn posts and beams; handmade wooden furniture,
hooked rugs and quilts. A 32'-high free-standing
stone fireplace chimney in the hexagonal "head
room" has 3 fireplaces. Opened in 1938, the $1
million building was dedicated by President Roosevelt after his dedication of Bonneville Dam.

13. ARCHEOLOGICAL DIG: One of the most outstanding archeological excavations in North America, at
Ozette Village, allows a look at native American
daily life of five centuries ago. The dig, which
attracted worldwide attention, was underway for 11
years, until 1981, at Washington's Cape Alava.
    The site was revealed in 1970 when severe
winter storms at this most westerly point of the
lower 48 washed out artifacts from a beach ledge.
Washington State University archeologists, led by
Dr. Richard Daugherty, found five 500-year-old
Makah Indian longhouses that had been flattened
and preserved by repeated mudslides from a hillside. The whale-hunting Makahs had lived at the
site, off and on, for several thousand years. Deposits that old at the Ozette site hold harpoon
barbs and bones from humpback and gray whales,
hunted in sea-going canoes carved of redcedar.
    Recovered from the community dwellings were
more than 60,000 artifacts, many of wood and fiber
including fragile matting. Claylike mud and water-
logging protected them from decay. Excavation of
one house alone required four years.
    500 of the choicest artifacts are displayed in

Neah Bay at the Makah Cultural and Research Center
museum, built in 1979, the only place outside of
WSU where the artifacts are displayed.

Inside the handsome museum is a full-size rep-
lica of a cedar long-house, with removable timbers
and planks. Because cedar easily splits straight,
the Makahs had dimensional lumber, very unusual
where there were no saws. Many wedges for split-
ting cedar were found, made of whalebone, antler,
yew wood, and even heavy black basalt, carried to
the Ozette beach by Ice Age glaciers.

Among the many artifacts found were 1000 mats,
hats and baskets made mostly of cedar bark; 11
cradles, suspended from the ceiling and rocked by
a cord; and an extraordinary blanket made of wood-
pecker feathers and dog hair mixed with cattail
tail fluff, interwoven with cedar bark.

*OZETTE VILLAGE ARCHEOLOGICAL EXCAVATION: from Northwest's most out-
standing dig, a 500-year-old cedar whale fin inlaid with 700
sea-otter teeth (Makah Cultural & Research Center)*

THE LARGEST

1. DOMED STADIUM: Seattle's Kingdome, finished in 1976, has the world's largest thin-shelled concrete dome and self-supporting roof, with no posts to interfere with spectator viewing. Forty perimeter columns, 52' apart, support roof and ramps. The top of the dome is 250' from the floor.

The West's first domed stadium, covering 9.1 acres, is located near the area Seattle pioneers settled in 1851, and near Skid Road, down which logs were skidded to Yesler's waterfront sawmill.

The record for a single event in the Kingdome was 74,000 who came in 1976 to hear Billy Graham. Perhaps the largest indoor party in the world was given there when Boeing's two-session Christmas party in 1980 brought 103,152 people.

SEATTLE'S KINGDOME: West's first domed stadium; world's largest self-supporting roof (The Kingdome)

2. BOOKSTORE: Seattle's University Book Store has the largest book sales volume of any of the 3000 college bookstores in the U.S., among the largest in the U.S. for all types of bookstores. The off-campus store has the Northwest's largest stock of current titles, and one of the nation's largest. In 1900 the store was on campus, run by students in a Denny Hall coat closet.

3. EDUCATION LEVEL: Washington has the highest level of education in the Northwest, 3rd in the U.S. with 77% of adults over 25 having completed high school. Nearly 1 in 4 Seattleites has gone to college. Washington has one of the nation's largest community college systems per capita-- 27 colleges, 83,000 full-time-equivalent students.

4. BUSINESS HEADQUARTERS: Boise has one of the largest concentrations per capita in the U.S. of world and national business headquarters. Among them are Morris Knudtson, world's largest heavy-construction company; Boise-Cascade, Albertson's, Ore-Ida, and J.R. Simplot Company.

5. OYSTERS: Washington has the largest Pacific oyster production on the West Coast. More than 90% of West Coast oysters are grown there, 5 times what Oregon and California together produce. Willapa Bay has the nation's largest oyster beds.

6. THEATRE: Seattle is second in the nation only to New York City in number of live theatre performances, in size of theatre company, and in number of actors employed by its eight most important theatres. Oldest (1962) and largest (850 seats) is Seattle Repertory Theatre, now performing in a new Seattle Center home, Bagley Wright Theatre.

7. BOOKSTORE: Seattle's Shorey's Bookstore is one of the nation's 3 largest antiquarian bookstores, one of the world's largest (with 1.5 million volumes) and Seattle's first used-book store, founded in 1890 shortly after the big fire.

8. SCIENCE MUSEUM: Seattle's Pacific Science Center has the nation's 2nd largest membership for a hands-on science museum; the Northwest's only IMAX theater, 60' wide and 3½ stories high; the only Northwest Indian long house, with original posts. The museum has one of the Northwest's most active educational programs with children's summer camps; four computer and science vans that go to schools and stay for days or weeks; and one of the nation's largest training programs for teachers in science, math, and computers. Its Creativity Exhibit, a hands-on program, is one of the nation's best. A Science Playground for both adults and children fills an entire building.

9. FERRY SYSTEM: The Washington State Ferry System is the largest in the Western Hemisphere. Its 22 ferries, traveling the world's most scenic waters, carried 17,127,846 passengers in 1985, and 7,021,906 vehicles.

Part of the state highway system, the ferries connect highways on 13 islands and 2 peninsulas. Once, ferries were a necessity on Lake Washington and Puget Sound. Puget Sound's first scheduled ferryboat, CITY OF SEATTLE, began service on New Year's Eve, 1888. The steam-driven side-wheeler ran from downtown Seattle to West Seattle.

The LESCHI, a side paddle-wheeler used in Lake Washington before the floating bridges, locks and ship canal, was built in Seattle, then dismantled, and finally put back together again in the lake.

Puget Sound's first motor ferry was the VASHON ISLAND, launched in June 1916. The early ferries

were operated by cities, counties and the Port of
Seattle. The KALAKALA, Puget Sound's first stream-
lined ferry and the first to have radar, was orig-
ginally the fire-ravaged PERALTA, a San Francisco
ferry rebuilt in Seattle as a single-ender.

On early open-deck ferries, cars shared space
with horse-drawn vehicles. Cars too high to go
through the low, narrow ferry entrances had their
tires deflated, and sometimes their tops and wind-
shields removed to make them fit. Shoved on and
later shoved off again, cars were reassembled on
shore, with tires inflated by hand pump.

The state entered the ferry business in 1951.
Lake Washington was bridged, but most island residents oppose bridges, and much of the Sound is
unbridgeable, except for the Tacoma Narrows. So,
ferries are part of the area's future, despite a
perpetual deficit and trouble-prone superferries.
In 1986 passenger-carrying catamarans were being
tested as an alternative to new auto ferries.

10. PLANNED CITY: Longview, Washington, was the West's largest and first completely planned city, the nation's second largest, next to Washington D.C. Long-Bell, the largest lumber company in the U.S. at that time, built Longview as a mill town in 1922 at a cost of $50 million. Located there now is the world's largest wood-products and pulp complex, owned by Weyerhaeuser.

Since Long-Bell needed a major deepwater port, it built Longview on the banks of the Columbia on the site of a former town, Monticello, destroyed earlier by a flood. The new town was protected by a $3.25 million dike 14 miles long and 300' wide at the base. It saved Longview from a disastrous flood in 1948 that damaged other cities.

11. TIMBER COMPANY: Weyerhaeuser Company is the world's largest single integrated manufacturer of forest products. Its Longview wood-products and pulp complex is the world's largest: sawmills, plywood plant, pulp and paperboard mill, chemical plant, bark products plant, and research center. The company is one of the top producers of soft-wood lumber, and the world's largest private owner of timber, the only major forest-products firm self-sufficient in timber land-- 6 million acres in 10 states, 46% of it in the Northwest.

Frederick Weyerhaeuser, who began in 1856 as a 21-year-old emigrant in an Illinois sawmill, came to the Northwest as owner of one of the largest company complexes in the Lake States. In 1900 in one of the biggest real estate deals in history, he bought 900,000 acres of Douglas fir forest from Great Northern Railroad-- at $6 an acre.

Although the company's $5 billion forest products business is its largest, it has diversified into mortgages, banks, nurseries, disposable diapers, hydroponic lettuce, and into real estate. In 1984 it was the nation's most profitable real estate company, worth $85 million.

12. PETROGLYPHS: One of the largest Indian petroglyphs in North America is carved on a lava rock on the Snake River's north shore south of Nampa. On Map Rock is carved a detailed map of the Snake River country, including Jackson Lake in Wyoming.

13. DOME: The Tacoma Dome is the world's largest wooden dome arena. The 15-story-high arena seats 256,000.

14. CAPITOL DOME: Olympia's capitol dome (1928) is the world's 4th largest at 287', exceeded only by domes in Washington D.C., St. Paul's in London and St. Peter's in Rome. It is one of only two U.S. domes built of solid masonry. Inside, 185' overhead, hangs a brass Tiffany chandelier.

OLYMPIA CAPITOL DOME: world's 4th largest, one of nation's only two solid masonry domes (Washington State Library)

15. JET PLANE: The Boeing Company produces the world's largest commercial jet airliner, the 747. It is taller than a five-story building, 63' 5". The 747 is assembled in the world's largest building (by volume), located adjacent to Paine Field in South Snohomish County.

Finished in 1966, the 115'-high building is 2068' wide and 1614' deep. Originally containing 200 million cu. ft., it was enlarged in 1980 to 291 million cu. ft. for production of the 767 twinjet. Major parts of manufacture, subassembly and final assembly take place under one roof.

In grading and leveling the 780-acre site, 4.7 million cubic yards of earth were moved, 1 1/2 times as much as in building Grand Coulee Dam. The 15-million-gallon holding pond built for runoff water could float an ocean-going ship. A 3-mile-long railroad spur that joins the site with mainline tracks 540' below is the nation's second steepest standard gauge railroad-- a 5.6% grade.

THE BOEING COMPANY: world's largest commercial jet airliner (747) is built in world's largest-volume building (The Boeing Company)

16. POWER TRANSMISSION: Bonneville Power Admin-
istration has the largest network of long-distance
high-voltage electric transmission lines in the
U.S.   BPA markets power from more than 20 multi-
purpose dams on the Columbia and its tributaries.
Upgrading of a direct-current, high-voltage transmission line in early 1986 from the Columbia River
to Los Angeles-- one of the longest such lines in
the world at 846 miles-- boosted power from 1600
to 2000 megawatts.

17. SAWMILL: Potlatch Sawmill, one of the largest sawmills in the world, is located on the Palouse River at Lewiston, Idaho. The lumber yard
alone covers 65 acres. The Potlatch Lumber Company, a subsidiary of Weyerhaeuser, which built
the huge mill, veneer and plywood plants, and
company town, owns thousands of acres of white
pine forest in northern Idaho. That state is one
of the leaders in the nation in forest crops.
    Annual log drives, the last in the U.S., on
the North Fork of the Clearwater River used to
bring logs to the sawmill pond. Throughout the
95-mile trip, loggers had to be alert, ready to
break up any log jams. The log drives ended with
the construction of Dworshak Dam in 1973, third
highest dam in the U.S. at 717 feet.

18. TROUT FARM: The world's largest single commercial trout farm is the Clear Springs Trout
Company in southcentral Idaho's Magic Valley between Twin Falls and Hagerman in the Thousand
Springs area. Owner Bob Erkins sells 12 million
trout a year, 40,000 a week to New York alone. 90%
of all trout bought in the U.S. come from this
area, where 50 trout farms thrive in a canyon 32
miles long. The secret is highly oxygenated 58-
degree water from the Snake River Aquifer flowing
constantly through fish-filled raceways.

19. ELEPHANTS: Portland's Washington Park Zoo has the largest breeding herd of Asian-elephants of any zoo in the world, and the world's most successful Asian-elephant rearing program. It all began with a gift to the zoo in 1953 of a 4-year-old elephant. In 1984 the herd numbered 11, with 3 males. Over the years the zoo has had 33 different elephants, 23 born at the zoo. Some have gone to circuses or zoos; a few have died.

Washington Park Zoo has become a respected international center of elephant knowledge. The first to establish the estrus cycle of Asian-elephants, they are leaders in developing an artificial insemination program. This is critical; export of the endangered Asian-elephants has been prohibited since 1975, and most zoos will not keep males, especially dangerous in breeding season.

Much of the zoo's success is due to its elephant facilities, designed to avoid handling and chaining. Unchained elephants are happier, and happier elephants breed more readily. Handling is avoided by the use of remote-control, hydraulically operated doors, and a unique "squeeze cage" with hydraulically operated walls that immobilize elephants for medication, avoiding sedation, which is always risky. The elephants have showers and a six-foot-deep, 80,000-gallon pool that holds three of the very sociable females at one time.

The zoo's Packy is the world's only second-generation, captive bull Asian-elephant to become a father-- 7 times. He is the largest Asian elephant in the Western Hemisphere, 6 tons, 10' tall. His father, Thonglaw, sired 15 calves before he died in 1974. The birth of Packy at the zoo in 1962, the first elephant zoo birth in the Western Hemisphere in 44 years, was carried live on TV. Packy mated with 20-year-old Rosy for the latest birth, April 1983. This was her 6th calf, a world record for babies born to a single captive elephant mother. After a birth the elephants trumpet noisily for hours.

20. CITY PARKS: Portland has the Northwest's largest city park system, with 163 parks totaling some 7500 acres. Among them is the largest wilderness forest area within the limits of a U.S. city-- Forest Park, 8 miles long and 1 1/2 miles wide with nearly 6000 acres and 50 miles of hiking trails. Logged in the past, it still has 300 acres of large trees and is now the most protected of any comparable forest land in the U.S. Like many of Portland's parks, it has superb views of mountains and rivers, especially from 22-room Pittock Mansion, at 1000' elevation.

Forest Park is part of Washington Park, the world's largest city park, which was the first parkland acquired (in 1871) after 3 large downtown parks were set aside by early city fathers as open space. (Of those, South Park extends 13 blocks along Park Avenue through Portland State U. campus; North Park's 6 blocks border a Skid Road district; Waterfront Park is 1 mile long.)

Washington Park has the most points of interest in Portland. It includes one of the most authentic Japanese Gardens in the world outside Japan, 5 1/2 acres with 5 traditional forms, an authentic pavilion, and a vista of Mount Hood.

High in the hills of Washington Park are 2500 varieties in the Rhododendron Test Gardens, and 8,000 rose bushes of 400 varieties in the International Rose Test Gardens. Its Rose Festival, begun in 1905, is one of the nation's five largest annual celebrations.

Washington Park Zoo is one of the oldest in the U.S., established on 61 acres in 1887. It has the world's largest captive herds of Asian-elephants, one of the few Penguinariums in the world, and one of the largest chimpanzee colonies in the nation.

North of the zoo is the Western Forestry Center, which replaced the center built for the 1905

Lewis and Clark Exposition. The new center is the best of its kind in the U.S. Among its features are a 70-foot "talking tree" and an exhibit that rekindles the Tillamook Burn of 1933.

Hoyt Arboretum, which connects Forest Park with Washington Park, has within its 216 acres of trees and trails 600 species of trees and shrubs, and one of the largest collections of distinct species of conifers of any U.S. arboretum.

Another outstanding attraction in Washington Park is the Oregon Museum of Science and Industry (OMSI), one of the nation's most distinguished. Its Kendall Planetarium gives shows twice a day, five times on week ends. Its 40' dome can project 5000 stars, planets, sun and moon. OMSI's many science and energy exhibits include a 14'-high, 22'-long Walk-Through Heart and a life-size Transparent Woman who talks about the human body. OMSI sponsors computer classes, summer camps, trips to a field station in fossil-rich John Day country, laboratory experiences, and science classes.

Portland's Mill Ends Park, the world's smallest park at 24" in diameter, was created downtown by a columnist on the OREGONIAN newspaper, and named after his column.

21. DAM: Grand Coulee Dam has the largest number of superlatives of any U.S. dam. It was the largest construction project ever undertaken in the world up to that time, larger than the Great Pyramid. It is the largest solid concrete dam in the world. 23.9 million tons (12 million barrels) of concrete were poured. Its record for pouring the most concrete in 24 hours still stands: 20,000 cubic yards

Grand Coulee impounds the largest body of water on the Columbia. Franklin D. Roosevelt Lake stretches 151 miles to the Canadian border.

In 1955 Grand Coulee lost to Russia its first place in the world in total production of hydro-

electric power, but regained it in 1970 by adding
a third powerhouse, which houses some of the
world's largest hydroelectric units-- 600,000 and
700,000 kilowatts. The turbine generators are the
largest of their kind in the world. Total hydroelectric potential when all 6 units are installed
in the third powerhouse will be 6,480,000 kilowatts. A gantry crane inside the new generating
plant is the world's most powerful.

Grand Coulee Dam made possible one of the
nation's largest irrigation projects--the Columbia Basin Project. Its impounded water irrigates
505,000 acres, and could irrigate more. 2300 miles
of canals and laterals channel the water to 6000
farms. Six of the world's largest pumps lift
water for irrigation 280' into Banks Lake, formed
by damming both ends of 27-mile-long Grand Coulee.

At its peak the dam provided 8800 jobs, the
largest Depression-era construction project.

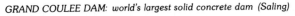

GRAND COULEE DAM: world's largest solid concrete dam (Saling)

22. WAGON TRAIN: The largest number of people to travel together in one train on the Oregon Trail involved nearly 1000 people in 1942, led by Marcus Whitman. No wagon train was ever so big again; smaller ones were more manageable. The largest number of emigrants traveled after 1849, when some 50,000 headed for California's goldfields, outnumbering Oregon farm-seekers 50 to 1.

The Oregon Trail was one of history's most famous emigrant routes, 1962 miles long. Not a single trail, the route varied by as much as 10 miles as groups sought to avoid grazed-out areas and dust, or looked for short-cuts. In the 1840s some 12,000 traveled the full distance.

The trail evolved gradually, very little of it due to Lewis and Clark's expedition. The Astorians in 1811-12 created part of it, and even more on a return trip. In the 1820s and 1830s mountain men used parts of the trail, some of them later acting as guides. The mass migration really began in 1841 when 69 people started out in a wagon train. In 1844 4000 set out; in 1845, 5000.

More than 20,000 are believed to have died on the way in the 20 years between 1840, when the first Oregon-bound emigrants crossed, and 1859. Usually the dead were buried in unmarked graves at the head of the next day's journey, so that wagon wheels rolling over the graves would conceal them.

Most of the emigrants walked the long trail, except for the very young and the ill. The oxen could not pull the extra weight for long, loaded as the wagons were with belongings and provisions for the trip and for the first year in Oregon.

Even after the emigrants reached The Dalles, there was a frightening trip ahead down the Columbia. Wagons were dismantled and lashed to rafts, then reassembled at the Cascades, and a portage made to today's Bonneville Dam. Again came dismantling and rafting down to the Willamette. Some who survived the 4- to 6-month overland trip drowned during the final part of the journey.

23. WINE: Washington is the nation's second biggest producer of vinifera grapes and premium wines second only to California. Wine-making has recently been one of its fastest-growing industries. In the early 1980s, wineries in all three Northwest states began to win gold and silver medals in regional, national and international competitions for such classic European wines as Chardonnay, Pinot Noir, Merlot, Cabernet Sauvignon and Riesling.

Although wine was made as early as 1872 on Washington's Stretch Island, and in Idaho in the 1860s near Lewiston, the Northwest wine industry was revitalized in the 1960s. In 1985 Washington alone harvested 17,100 tons of wine grapes, producing 2.6 million gallons of varietal wines. The grapes got the highest average price per ton in the U.S.-- $573, compared to California's $185.

In 1985 there were more than 120 active Northwest wineries, some 60 in Washington, which has the Northwest's most acreage in vinifera grapes- 11,000 acres in 1985. Most are grown in south-central Washington. More than half the state's wine-grape acreage belongs to its largest winery, Chateau Ste. Michelle, the nation's second largest producer of premium wines.

Yakima Valley in 1983 was the first Northwest area to receive federal recognition as a distinct and official viticultural area. Walla Walla and Columbia Valleys also have been so honored.

Oregon's 50 wineries are often family-style operations, 5 to 20 acres, mostly in western Oregon, and often growing Pinot Noir grapes. Ste. Chapelle in Idaho, which has 6 wineries, is the second largest Northwest winery. Idaho's wine grapes grow mostly in the southwest, some at 3000', highest altitude of any Northwest grape.

All 3 states have nearly ideal conditions for wine-grape growing: sandy loam over rocky volcanic soil for good drainage and heat retention; 2 hours more light each summer day than in California; and cool nights that give a desirable tartness.

23. FISH HATCHERY: The Dworshak National Fish Hatchery on Idaho's Clearwater River is one of the world's largest steelhead trout hatcheries. Since Dworshak Dam keeps steelhead from their spawning grounds on the North Fork, the hatchery compensates for the loss by raising each year 3 million steelhead, 1.5 million rainbow trout. One million Chinook salmon are also raised, for losses caused by dams on the lower Snake.

24. EXPORTER: The Boeing Company is the nation's largest exporter, and the Northwest's largest employer. In March 1986 the company received the largest order for aircraft in aviation history: $3.3 billion for 14 747-400s plus 6 options. That same month Boeing made an unprecedented move, taking Japan as a 25% partner in the development and production of the 7J7, a new 150-seat airplane.

25. SILVER MINE: The nation's largest silver mine is Idaho's Sunshine Mine. One mile deep with 100 miles of tunnels, it was the site of the world's worst hardrock mine disaster when, in 1972, fire spread carbon monoxide and smoke through the tunnels, killing 91 of 176 miners.

26. HYDROELECTRIC PLANTS: Of the 30 largest hydroelectric plants in the U.S., 4 are in Oregon, 12 in Washington. Those 16 include the top 3: Grand Coulee, John Day, and Chief Joseph Dams.

27. STATUE: Portland has the Northwest's largest hammered-copper sculpture, second in size in the U.S. only to the Statue of Liberty. Portlandia, a kneeling female figure nearly 35 feet tall and weighing 6 1/2 tons, took her place in front of the Portland Building in October 1985.

THE FIRST OR OLDEST

1. WOMEN TRAVELERS: The first two women to travel across the continent were missionary wives Narcissa Whitman and Eliza Spalding. The Whitmans built the first American home in today's Washington that was not a trading post, on the banks of the Walla Walla River in 1836. The Spaldings settled in Idaho near Lapwai Creek, building Idaho's first home in 1837. The first white child born in the Northwest was the Whitman's daughter, who drowned when she was two. In 1847 while nursing Indians sick from a measles epidemic, the Whitmans and 12 others in the Mission were massacred by Indians who thought they had been poisoned.

2. FIRST SETTLEMENT: The first European settlement in the Northwest was in 1792 at Fort Nuñez Gaona in today's Neah Bay. It was intended to be a provisioning depot for Spanish ships. Headed by Lt. Salvador Fidalgo, the settlement consisted of 10 log cabins inside a stockade, with a forge and brick ovens for baking bread. Pigs, cattle and sheep were brought from Mexico, and a vegetable garden was planted. The venture lasted only four months before Britain forced Spain out of all land north of San Francisco.

3. PAVED ROAD: The Northwest's first paved road, the Columbia Gorge Scenic Highway, was completed in 1915 before there were many cars in the area. Replacing paths and cattle trails, it followed one of the most historic and scenic routes in the region. Indians, Lewis and Clark, then Oregon Trail emigrants had all traveled parts of the old route as they were forced to portage around impassable rapids in the Columbia.
    The two-lane paved road, 24 feet wide, was an

engineering miracle. Although the road was built on very steep slopes, the grade was never more than 5 degrees. Even with as many as five switchbacks, the curves were easy to drive. Stonemasons brought from Italy used local basalt to build drywall masonry walls and guardrails, some 12' thick at the base and up to 26' high. Mitchell Tunnel, blasted through solid rock, offered views of the river framed by open arches.

Until 1950 this scenic road was the only route along the Oregon side of the Columbia, the main route to The Dalles. Today, a modern freeway runs close to the river, but some 40 miles of the old scenic highway are still open, passing near many spectacular waterfalls. 720 feet above the river, Crown Point Vista House offers superb views.

4. BUILDING: Washington's oldest standing structure is the Fort Nisqually granary, built in 1843 and now a National Historic Landmark. The fort was the first permanent white settlement and port on Puget Sound, and the most northerly British fur-trading post in Oregon Country. The granary and Chief Factor's House (1854) are among the very few original buildings remaining in the U.S. from the fur-trading era.

90% of the granary is original. It survived because it was built solidly of heavy squared logs in the post-on-sill style used at Hudson's Bay Company forts. 30% of the Chief Factor's house is original, including a 60-foot-long timber.

Several Fort Nisquallys existed at different locations-- in 1833, a store and a cedar hut down on the delta; then, a dwelling and store on the bluff, later replaced by larger buildings. In 1843 the final fort, with some 20 buildings, was built near a creek a mile inland.

Fort Nisqually continued to operate even after the Canadian-American boundary treaty in 1846. HBC sold the fort to the U.S. government in 1869. The

FORT NISQUALLY GRANARY: Washington's oldest standing structure (1843) in first permanent European settlement on Puget Sound (Tacoma Metropolitan Park District)

last Factor became an American citizen and took over the fort. After he died in 1906, Dupont Powder Company bought the land with the two historic buildings on it. During expansion plans in 1933, Dupont planned to tear down the granary. But that was the year of the Fort Nisqually Centennial. So, the two buildings were removed and rebuilt in 1934 in Point Defiance Park. Soon after, the entire fort was reconstructed to original specifications from lumber cut at the site and finished by old methods. One section of the stockade is original.

5. MISSION: The Northwest's two oldest buildings were built by Oregon's first missionary. Jason Lee House and the Parsonage (c. 1841) are now displayed in Salem near the Capitol. Lee's first Methodist mission, built in 1834, was a failure. He returned to the East for more recruits, and 52 came out in 1840.

Lee then established Chemeketa Methodist Mission 10 miles upstream from the old one. A controversial man, he was recalled in 1844.

6. MISSION: Idaho's Cataldo Mission, completed in 1853, is the oldest building in Idaho, a National Historic Landmark. Annual flooding of the first mission, built of logs in 1842 on the banks of the St. Joe River, forced a move 30 miles east of Coeur d'Alene. There, the new mission, 40 by 40 by 90 feet, was built by Coeur d'Alene Indians, supervised by Father Anthony Ravalli. They used only broad axe, auger, ropes and pulleys, and penknife. Interior wall timbers 22" square and 20' long were hewn and planed with a broad axe. The outside walls were insulated with woven straw or grass covered with river-bank mud.

Later, carvings, paintings and 6 columns were added. Also in the complex were a parsonage, parish hall, grist mill, and cabin. Cataldo Mission was a major center for Indian activity and learning but was abandoned in 1887. It was restored in 1928. Indians attend a Mass said there each year.

CATALDO SACRED HEART MISSION: Idaho's oldest standing building (1853) (Idaho Travel Council)

7. UNIVERSITY: Oregon Institute was the North-west's first private institution of higher learn-ing. In 1842 it bought the land and buildings of Jason Lee's Chemeketa Mission school. Eventually it merged with Salem's Willamette University, the Northwest's oldest existing institution of higher education, chartered in 1853.

The Congregational Church in 1849 established Tualatin Academy at Forest Grove; it is now Paci-fic University, chartered in 1854. For 100 years until 1948, Old College Hall on its campus was the oldest building in use for higher education west of the Mississippi. Old College Hall was the first frame building on Tualatin Plains.

8. WOOD CARVING: The oldest wood carving ever found on the Northwest coast, 2750 years old, was discovered in 1983 at the mouth of the Hoko River on the Olympic Peninsula. A water-saturated river bank preserved the 5 1/2"-high cedar carving, per-haps a weaving tool handle, 1000 years older than any earlier find. Thousands of artifacts have been found at the former Makah fishing camp.

9. HOME: One of the Northwest's oldest homes, built in Oregon City in 1846, was the retirement home of Dr. John McLoughlin, Chief Fac-tor of Fort Vancouver for 20 years. Oregon City was the first  incorporated city west of the Rockies, the North-west's largest city in the 1840s, a center of gov-ernment. In 1828 McLoughlin chose the Willamette Falls as the site for the first Northwest's first sawmill. A town began to form near the base of

the 41' falls, site of the Northwest's first
locks. With mill employees and emigrants diverted
south, the town had 30 buildings by the winter of
1842. A transportation industry developed to
portage cargo and passengers around the falls to
upstream settlements. The first post offices in
Oregon Country were established in 1847 at Oregon
City and Astoria. Oregon's first covered bridge
was built there in 1851. McLoughlin retired to
and died in the city by the falls.

10. LIGHTHOUSE: The oldest operating lighthouse
in the Northwest is Cape Disappointment at the
north side of the treacherous Columbia River bar.
Some 230 ships have been wrecked near the Cape.
Given first priority in the Northwest for navigational aids, the lighthouse began operating in
1856 after years of delays. The beacon in the 53'-

CAPE DISAPPOINTMENT LIGHTHOUSE: Northwest's oldest lighthouse (1856);
north side of treacherous Columbia River bar (U.S. Coast Guard)

tower 220' above sea level, is visible for 22
miles. Before it was built, Indians sighting a
ship paddled a canoe to Astoria and brought back
volunteers, who then hiked 12 miles up the Cape.
At night the warning to the ships was a bonfire;
during the day, white cloths tied to trees.

11. FARMERS' MARKET: The nation's oldest continuously operating farmers' market is Seattle's Pike
Place Market, started in August 1907. An 1896
City Council ordinance authorizing a public market
wasn't implemented until the Northwest lumber boom
resulting from San Francisco's earthquake and fire
in 1906 sent food prices soaring. Middle-men com-
mission houses underpaid farmers and overcharged
consumers. The solution was a farmers' market.

Pike Place Market was an instant success. On
the first Saturday, 50 customers were waiting before the farmers' wagons appeared. Everything
sold quickly. The next Saturday 70 wagons showed
up. From then on, buyers poured in on Saturdays,
by street car, carriage, foot and bicycle. Some
came from small waterfront communities aboard
Mosquito Fleet boats, both to buy and to sell.

King County once had more than 3000 farms,
many run by European or Asian emigrants, and Puget
Island farms were also numerous. The filling of
tideflat land as part of the Denny Regrade, perhaps the most extensive recontouring project any
U.S. city ever undertook, provided an ideal market
location on the waterfront.

At the market's peak in 1939, 515 licenses for
farmer-vendors were issued; in 1949, only 53-- the
result of Japanese farmers having to give up their
land during World War II. Customers were fewer
because of post-war competition from frozen foods,
supermarkets, and refrigerated trucks bringing in
produce from other areas. As First Avenue became
a skid-road area, market facilities deteriorated,
making shopping there unattractive.

*PIKE PLACE MARKET-- c. 1910: nation's oldest continuously operating
Farmers' Market (U.W. Libraries, Historical Photography Collection)*

In 1950 suggestions were made to demolish the market and build a 7-story garage on the site. As the plans escalated in scope each year, worried market merchants and farmers formed an association in 1956. Artist Mark Tobey and architect Victor Steinbrueck led a long fight to save the market.

In 1971 Seattle voters approved an initiative to fund renovation of the market, which had been declared a National Historical District.

Controversy continues in the 1980s, as crafts-persons and trendy shops far outnumber farmers.

12. LAWS: Oregon has consistently been one of the first in the U.S. to pass progressive legislation benefitting its people. In 1902 it passed a constitutional amendment allowing the initiative and referendum, adding a direct presidential primary in 1904, and the recall in 1908.

"Oregon System" school laws were the first in

the U.S. authorizing state-printed texts. In 1912 Oregon began compulsory education.

It had early laws requiring public access to ocean beaches at least every 3 miles and preventing the taking of marine animals from beaches except with a research permit

In 1913 Oregon passed laws for workmen's compensation and widows' pensions. In 1930 Public Utility Districts were authorized to generate and sell electricity. Oregon passed a Fair Employment Act in 1949. It was the first state to ban fluorocarbons in aerosol spray cans (1977).

Its litter and bottle-return law was the nation's first. In 1983 it was the first state to set pollution-emission limits on wood stoves.

FISH WHEEL: first used on the Columbia, to catch salmon for commercial canning (Oregon Historical Society- C.E. Watkins)

13. FISHWHEELS: The fishwheel was first used on the Columbia River. Invented in 1879, they were inspired by the Columbia's huge salmon runs and the growing industry of canning salmon. Most were operated by three Columbia Gorge canneries.

Permanent or floating, the 30' wheels were powered by river current. They harvested tons of

salmon effortlessly, with wire-covered baskets
scooping them up and dumping them into boxes.
They were too efficient and too numerous, drastically cutting salmon runs. Oregon outlawed them in
1927, Washington in 1934.

*FIRST INTERNATIONAL AIRMAIL FLIGHT-- 1919: Canada to Seattle's Lake
Union; pilot Eddie Hubbard (l.), William E. Boeing Sr. (r.)
founder of the Boeing Company (The Boeing Company Archives)*

14. AIRMAIL: The first international airmail was
flown on March 3, 1919 from Canada near the Royal
Vancouver Yacht Club to Seattle's Lake Union. The
passenger in the fabric-covered, pontoon-equipped
C-700 seaplane was William E. Boeing Sr., founder
of Seattle's new Boeing Airplane Company. It was
the first flight over the Canadian border west of
the Great Lakes.

Bringing back a sack of 60 letters was not the
inauguration of scheduled international airmail
service, but rather, a publicity stunt for the
Vancouver War Trophies Exhibition that Boeing had
visited. The flight was, however, a notable
"first" in Pacific Northwest aviation history.

15. WORLD'S FAIR: Seattle's Century 21, North America's first space-age world's fair, was the first world's fair to make a profit. And it left a valuable legacy: 74-acre Seattle Center with graceful Gothic arches, fountains and parklike grounds, Coliseum, Pacific Science Center, Seattle Rep Theatre, refurbished opera house, a monorail train unusual in being part of a city transportation system, and the 605'-high Space Needle.

An earlier Seattle exposition also made a profit and left a legacy. The Alaska-Yukon-Pacific Exposition (1909) was held on the heavily wooded new campus of the University of Washington, whose regents hoped to benefit by land clearing and some permanent buildings. At the time it had only a dormitory, a canoe house and science building (now Parrington). A-Y-P legacy: Meany and Bagley Halls, Drumheller Fountain, and Campus Parkway.

SPACE NEEDLE: legacy of Seattle's 1962 World's Fair, North America's first profitable world's fair (Seattle Chamber of Commerce)

16. NEWSPAPER: The Northwest's oldest continuously operated newspaper is the <u>Oregonian</u>. It began in 1850 as a weekly, changing to a daily in 1861. Second oldest is <u>The Oregon Statesman</u>, (1851), the Northwest's most peripatetic, moving with Oregon's capital-- Oregon City, Salem, Corvallis, back to Salem-- never missing an issue.

17. COMPANY TOWN: The first company town in the Northwest was Port Gamble, founded in 1853 as a lumber town by Capt. William Talbot and Andrew Pope. They built a sawmill with material bought from Yesler's mill in Seattle. The original Puget Mill Company sawmill is still operating, oldest continuously operating sawmill in the Northwest, and one of the oldest in the U.S. Port Gamble's General Store, built in 1853, is still in use.

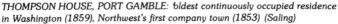

THOMPSON HOUSE, PORT GAMBLE: bldest continuously occupied residence in Washington (1859), Northwest's first company town (1853) (Saling)

18. IDAHO SETTLEMENT: The oldest permanent white settlement in Idaho was in Franklin, just across the border from Utah. Dating from April 1860, it was part of the Mormon expansion plan, but the colonists thought they were still in Utah.

FRANKLIN HOUSE: Idaho's oldest home (1860) in the state's oldest permanent European settlement (Idaho Travel Council)

19. FORT VANCOUVER FIRSTS: Since Fort Vancouver was established in 1825, it had many Northwest firsts: first bakery, chemist, blacksmith, wool growing, school, wheelwright, chapel, tinner, horticulture, gunpowder magazine, farming, dairying, saw and grist mills, library, hospital. It also began the first foreign trade, with Hawaii, Russian Alaska, and Mexican California.

20. AGRICULTURE: Oregon ranks first in the U.S. in production of peppermint (53.4% of the total crop), filberts (98.4%), prunes and plums (50.4%), grass seed (66%), Easter lily bulbs (90%), lumber products, and Christmas trees. Cattle and calves are Oregon's most valuable commodity.

21. AGRICULTURE: Washington is first in the U.S. in spearmint oil, dry edible peas, raspberries, Concord grapes, asparagus, sweet cherries, apples, and hops (producing 90% of hops used in U.S. beer making). It has the world's largest hop field, 790 acres, in Toppenish. Its cows give the top milk production per cow in the U.S. Washington and Idaho grow the most lentils in the U.S. Wheat is Washington's most valuable commodity.

22. POTATOES: Idaho ranks first in the nation in number of acres planted in potatoes and in total production. Washington has the world's highest yield per acre, with Oregon second. Idaho's potato processing industry is the nation's largest, handling 2/3 of all U.S. processed potatoes.

23. FORT FIRSTS: Fort Nisqually had the first: commercial enterprise in Puget Sound Country, white couple married, steamship on the Pacific, murder trial, 4th of July celebrated west of the Mississippi, and day-by-day record kept of early Puget Sound life. The daily Journal of Occurrences kept by Chief Factors from 1833 on is the oldest known account of life in that era.

24. GOLD BOOM TOWN: In 1852 Jacksonville was Oregon Territory's first gold boom town, richest of the Siskiyou mining camps. Some 80 historic mid-19th-century buildings of wood and brick are dated and marked in its National Historic Landmark District. Jacksonville was the first Rogue River Valley settlement, and the most important town in southern Oregon in the late 1890s, until bypassed by the railroad. Beekman Bank (1863) handled $31 million in gold in 17 years. Oldest buildings include Methodist (1854) and Catholic (1856) churches, butcher shop (1854), Drum Hotel (1858). In 1862 Peter Britt opened the Northwest's first photographic studio; he was the first to photograph Crater Lake (1874).

25. STEAMSHIP: The first steamship on the Columbia was the BEAVER, built on the Thames in 1835.
She came around the Horn, arriving under sail at
the Columbia River in 1836, paddle wheels on deck.
Copper-sheathed with a wooden hull, the BEAVER was
101.4' long with a 20'beam and 11' draft.

Sir George Simpson of Hudson's Bay Company re-
quested a ship, so that the British would be "mas-
ters of the trade" in Oregon Country.

Each spring the BEAVER steamed to Sitka with
supplies, picking up furs; it took stock to Vancouver Island and furs to Fort Vancouver; mail and
supplies from Fort Nisqually to outlying coastal
HBC stations. It stopped at Indian villages to
trade for furs, bartering knives, guns and cloth.

The wood-burning steamship required 40 cords
of wood a day. Every other day the crew had to go
ashore to cut wood, plentiful along the coast.

The BEAVER was active for 47 years, until it
broke up on rocks in 1883.

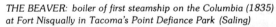

THE BEAVER: boiler of first steamship on the Columbia (1835)
at Fort Nisqually in Tacoma's Point Defiance Park (Saling)

26. RESIDENCE: The first house built north of the Columbia by an American citizen, and Washington's oldest residence, is a peeled-log cabin, the John R. Jackson House, at Mary's Corner near Chehalis, Washington. Built in 1844, it was often visited by emigrants heading north. Jackson, a representative in the first territorial legislature, entertained Grant, Sherman and McClellan there. In 1851 the house became the first federal district courthouse north of the Columbia.

JOHN JACKSON HOUSE: first house built north of the Columbia River and oldest residence of an American citizen (1844) (Saling)

27. FORT: Fort Astoria, the first American fort at the mouth of the Columbia, was the first commercial fur-trading post within today's Oregon, and the first permanent white settlement in the Northwest. John Jacob Astor of the Pacific Fur Company sent two parties, one overland, one around the Horn, to establish the post. The ship arrived first, in 1811, and Fort Astoria was built.

Sold to the North West Company during the War of 1812 by Astor's field partners, it became HBC Fort George when the two fur-trading companies merged. In 1825 HBC built Fort Vancouver on the more strategically located north side of the Columbia, and Fort George was abandoned.

Alt, David D., and Hyndman, Donald W, 1981, ROADSIDE GEOLOGY OF OREGON; 1984, ROADSIDE GEOLOGY OF WASHINGTON, Mountain Press, Missoula.

Armstrong, Robert H, 1980, A GUIDE TO THE BIRDS OF ALASKA, Alaska Northwest Publishing, Anchorage.

Arno, Stephen F., 1977, NORTHWEST TREES, Art by Ramona Hammerly, The Mountaineers, Seattle.

Buchsbaum, Ralph, 1950, ANIMALS WITHOUT BACKBONES, University of Chicago Press, Chicago.

Clark, Lewis J., 1976, WILD FLOWERS OF THE PACIFIC NORTHWEST, John G. Trelawny, ed., Gray's Publishing, Sidney, B.C.

Demoro, Harre, 1971, THE EVERGREEN FLEET, Golden West Books, San Marino, California.

Doerper, John, 1984, EATING WELL; 1985, SHELLFISH COOKERY, Pacific Search Press, Seattle

Fodor:FAR WEST: CALIFORNIA, WASHINGTON, OREGON, David McKay NY

Guinness Book of World Records.

Guberlet, Muriel, 1962, ANIMALS OF THE SEASHORE, Binfords & Mort, Portland, Oregon.

Gunther, Erna, 1973, ETHNOBOTANY OF WESTERN WASHINGTON, University of Washington Press, Seattle.

Harris, Stephen L., 1976, FIRE AND ICE: THE CASCADE VOLCANOES, The Mountaineers and Pacific Search Books, Seattle.

Holbrook, Stewart, Jones, Nard, and Haig-Brown, Roderick, 1963 THE PACIFIC NORTHWEST, Doubleday, Garden City, New York.

Kirk, Ruth, 1968, EXPLORING MOUNT RAINIER; 1964, EXPLORING THE OLYMPIC PENINSULA; 1974, WASHINGTON STATE NATIONAL PARKS, HISTORIC SITES, RECREATIONAL AREAS AND NATIONAL LANDMARKS; all by University of Washington Press, Seattle.

Kirk, Ruth, 1970, THE OLDEST MAN IN AMERICA: AN ADVENTURE IN ARCHAEOLOGY, Harcourt, Brace, Jovanovich, New York.

Kirk, Ruth, and Namkung, Johsel, 1973, THE OLYMPIC RAIN FOREST, University of Washington Press, Seattle.

Kozloff, Eugene N., 1976, PLANTS AND ANIMALS OF THE PACIFIC NORTHWEST; 1983, SEASHORE LIFE OF THE NORTHERN PACIFIC COAST; University of Washington Press, Seattle.

Krell, Dorothy, THE BEAUTIFUL NORTHWEST, Sunset Books, Lane Magazine & Book Co., Menlo Park, California.

Larrison, Earl J., 1976, MAMMALS OF THE NORTHWEST; 1970, WASHINGTON MAMMALS: THEIR HABITS, IDENTIFICATION AND DISTRIBUTION, Seattle Audubon Society, Seattle.

McKee, Bates, 1972, CASCADIA: GEOLOGIC EVOLUTION OF THE PACIFIC NORTHWEST, McGraw Hill, New York.

Niehaus, Theodore F., 1976, A FIELD GUIDE TO PACIFIC STATES WILDFLOWERS, Houghton Mifflin, Boston.

Plumb, Gregory, 1983, WATERFALLS OF THE PACIFIC NORTHWEST, The Writing Works, Seattle.

Ricketts, Edward, & Calvin, Jack, 1978, BETWEEN PACIFIC TIDES, Rev. by Joel W. Hedgpeth, Stanford University Press.

Scheffer, Victor B., 1980, ADVENTURES OF A ZOOLOGIST, Scribner

Scheffer, Victor B., 1984, THE SPIRES OF FORM, University of Washington Press, Seattle.

Shorett, Alice, and Morgan, Murray, 1982, THE PIKE PLACE MAR-KET, Pacific Search Press, Seattle.

Smith, Lynwood S., 1976, LIVING SHORES OF THE PACIFIC NORTH-WEST, Photos by Bernard Nist, Pacific Search Books, Seattle.

Speidel, Bill, 1974, THE WET SIDE OF THE MOUNTAINS, Nettle Creek Publishing, Seattle.

Spring, Ira, and Manning, Harvey, 1981, NORTHWEST OUTDOOR VACATION GUIDE, The Writing Works, Seattle.

Swartz, Susan, 1983, NATURE IN THE NORTHWEST, Photos by Bob & Ira Spring, Prentice Hall, Inglewood Cliffs, N.J.

SUNSET TRAVEL GUIDE TO IDAHO, 1972; SUNSET TRAVEL GUIDE TO OREGON, 1983, Lane Books, Menlo Park,CA.

Time-Life Books, THE PACIFIC STATES: CALIFORNIA, OREGON, WASHINGTON, Time-Life Library of America.

Time-Life Books, 1977, THE SNAKE RIVER COUNTRY, editor: Don Moser, Time-Life Library of America.

Whitney, Stephen, 1983, A FIELD GUIDE TO THE CASCADES AND OLYMPICS, The Mountaineers, Seattle.

Woodbridge, Sally, and Roger Montgomery, 1980, A GUIDE TO ARCHITECTURE IN WASHINGTON STATE, U. OF WASHINGTON PRESS.

WORLD ALMANAC AND BOOK OF FACTS, 1985.

Magazines, various issues: Sunset, Pacific Search, Northwest Edition, Pacific Northwest.

INDEX

OTHER BOOKS FROM ANSAL PRESS